Diary
Notebook

Joyce Jenje-Makwenda
Collection Archives

Featuring
WOMEN POLITICIANS/PARLIAMENTARIANS OF ZIMBABWE

This Diary was first published in 2012.
Second Edition 2017

ISBN 978-0-7974-6259-5

© Joyce Jenje Makwenda
Joyce Jenje Makwenda Collection Archive (JJMCA)
Women of Africa Diary
18 Wessex Drive
Mabelreign
HARARE
Zimbabwe
Tel: + 263-4-306623/306336
Cell: + 263 -773 468 378
Email: joycejenje@gmail.com
Website: www.joycejenjearchives.co.zw

WOMEN POLITICIANS/
PARLIAMENTARIANS
OF ZIMBABWE

Joyce Jenje Makwenda presents
Women Politicians/Parliamentarians of Zimbabwe

1800

NEHANDA
NYAKASIKANA

Queen Lozikeyi

Personal Details

Name   : ....

Address   : ....

                        ....

                        ....

Home Telephone Number : .... Fax..

Work Telephone Number : .... Fax..

Identity Number   : ....

Passport Number   : ....

Driving License No.   : ....

Car Registration Number   : ....

Insurance Policy Number   : ....

Bank Account Number   : ....

Medical Doctor   : ....

Dentist   : ....

Holistic Practitioner   : ....

Pharmacy   : ....

Allergies   : ....

Blood Group   : ....

Medical Aid No   : ....

Lawyer   : ....

YEAR PLANNER

JANUARY

FEBRUARY

MARCH

APRIL

MAY

JUNE

YEAR PLANNER

JULY

AUGUST

SEPTEMBER

OCTOBER

NOVEMBER

DECEMBER

Preface

THE DIARY NOTEBOOK celebrates many unsung heroines among women of Africa in the field of politics, leadership, sport, media, art, sculpture, activism, business entrepreneurship, and education.
It celebrates women from all sphere of life who make changes in their communities or countries, and who by so doing, inspire other women. The Diary challenges media stereotypes which see women as recipients of services, rather than providers of services. It is written in a simple way, it is entertaining and informative, and can be enjoyed while jotting an appointment, thus also encouraging the culture of reading.

The Women Politicians/Parliamentarians Diary Notebook chronicles the journey of women politicians since the 1800 to today. Some of the women featured are Modjadji, Nehanda, Lozikeyi, Muriel Rosin, Ruth Chinamano and most of the politicians and parliamentarians during the Government of National Unity 2008.

We should use as many ways as possible to document the histories of women for posterity and also disseminate stories.

Read on.....

JANUARY

SUN	MON	TUES	WED	THUR	FRI	SAT

BHUDHA Masara Sibusisiwe (MDC –T)

SIBUSISIWE Bhudha was born in 1971 in Kwekwe. She became involved in politics in 1999 first as a member of the National Constitutional Assembly. She believes in participation to effect change in governance. She says that she realized when she campaigned for the MDC, they were campaigning for men. "We thank organizations like WIPSU and the Women's Trust which has opened our minds as women, we are well informed."

The road to politics has been rough for her because of male domination and violence. In 2005 Matabeleland north failed to get a female MP because of patriarchy, "we could not do it as women because of economic power" she says. "We continued to campaign for men. In 2005 the party split, I was still in the National Assembly and the leader was allowed to be in the main body but most decisions were led by men. Women could not move motions...".

About achieving 50/50 representation, she believes that it must start at the lowest level. "In 2009 I was promised governorship but some of our big people were not happy and I was not sworn in, women in my party seem not to be worried that I haven't been sworn in," she says. She concludes by saying that women should rise above party politics and consider seriously how to achieve out 50/50 representation. Sibusisiwe does not believe in riding on men's backs for recognition.

NOTES

NOTES

NOTES

NOTES

NOTES

BHUKA Flora (ZANU PF - Minister of State for Special Affairs Responsible for Lands, Land Reform and Resettlement since 2005- MP Gokwe / Nembudziya)

FLORA BHUKA was born on 25 February 1968. She represents Gokwe-Nembudziya Constituency in the House of Assembly on a ZANU PF ticket. She did her secondary education at Loreto High School (1982-1985) and proceeded to St. Anthony`s High School for her 'A' levels (1986-1987). She attained a B.A. General Degree from the University of Zimbabwe (UZ) in 1990. In 1988, she was co-opted into Nyanje Youth District as Secretary for Administration after being identified as an active youth in the Gokwe University Students Association, an organization which sourced donations for schools and carried out research on socio-economic issues in Gokwe. She was elected Provincial Deputy Secretary for Transport and Welfare in the Youth League in 1993. In 1998 she was elected Provincial Secretary for the Commissariat in the Women`s League. She was appointed Constitutional Commissioner during the Constitutional Reform Process in 1999. She was also appointed to the Central Committee in 2001. She became National Secretary for Gender and Culture in the Women`s League in 2004.

She was elected Member of Parliament for Gokwe East in 2000, and was subsequently appointed Minister of State in the Office of the Vice President, responsible for the Land Reform Programme. She became the Chairperson of the Zimbabwe Women`s Caucus in 2001, an Executive Member of SADC Regional Women`s Caucus in 2002 and an Executive Member of the SADC Parliamentary Forum in 2004. In the March 2005 elections she retained her constituency and was subsequently appointed Minister of State for Special Affairs, responsible for the Land and Resettlement Programme. She was re-elected into the House of Assembly during the March 2008 elections to represent Gokwe-Nembudziya constituency, and was appointed Minister of State in the Vice President's office.

**CHABUKA Keresenzia
(MDC –T Deputy
Chairwoman of the Women
Parliamentarian Caucus –
Senator for Mutare)**

KERESENZIA Chabuka joined the MDC in 1999, and helped to set up MDC structures in Mutare. She was elected ward Chairwoman before she became Chairwoman for Manicaland Province and a Senator. She wants 50% representation for women in parliament, and encourages middle class women to engage in politics as everyone is affected by political decisions.

The civil society needs to educate people at grassroots level on the benefits of equal representation, and appreciates that women occupy the positions of Vice President and Deputy Prime Minister. She sees the 'pull-her-down syndrome' from fellow women as an obstacle to women empowerment. The media can also play a role to fully covering women projects.

She enjoys the support of her husband.

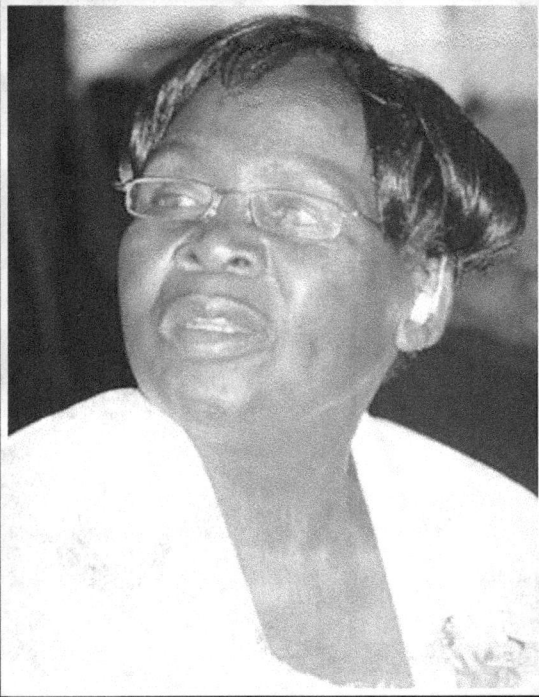

**CHADEROPA Fungai
(ZANU PF - MP Sanyati
Constituency)**

FUNGAI Chaderopa was born in 1949 and grew up in Bulawayo before her family moved to Nembudziya (Sanyati). In 1980 she became Zanu PF Chairwoman for Chenjiri for two years, and MP in 2008. Her husband is also a politician and very supportive.

She discourages MPs from engaging in partisan politics, which hinders development. The main hurdle for many aspiring female politicians is inter-party politics (de-campaigning each other), violence and men using beer (intoxicating youths) to campaign, which leads to violent campaigns.

Fungai is buying roofing and painting for schools in her constituency, and wants to repair the clinic at Chenjiri which was built by donors using boards that are now dilapidated. She wants more women to become councilors, and when they leave their positions they should be replaced by women and not men.

She advocates for better pay for civil servants and recognition of village health workers who work very hard. She wants more young people to join politics but to desist from violence.

**CHIBHAGU Gertrude
(ZANU PF - Senator for
Guruve-Mbire)**

GERTRUDE Chibhagu started political activism soon after independence. She worked for Mashonaland Central Province for 31 years, and was chosen by the people; men, women, and youths, to represent them as a Senator. She stood against four other women at Primaries, but won. She campaigned on foot, carrying a bottle of water (to quench thirst), and a packet of roasted dry maize (maputi). The constituency was reserved for women to achieve gender balance. Gertrude believes she won because she has a good working relationship with people of all background; rich and poor, in her area. She initiated community development projects in the Lower Valley; building new schools, improving agriculture and introducing cash crops such as cotton. Because of her good work with people, she also won 1 706 from the Doma people (Bushmen) who generally do not want to see people from outside their community. She is also upgrading women's lives, and has four female councilors in Upper Guruve. She believes that there should be more women in parliament and decision-making positions because they work hard for their constituencies.

Gertrude Chibhagu gets support from her husband, who encourages her projects. She says being in Parliament has been an eye-opener for her. It proves that anyone, especially women, can achieve anything. She was educated by her brother after her father refused to buy her books, and believed in educating boys. In Parliament she is confident to move any motion as long she is representing the wishes of her people.

FEBRUARY

SUN	MON	TUES	WED	THUR	FRI	SAT

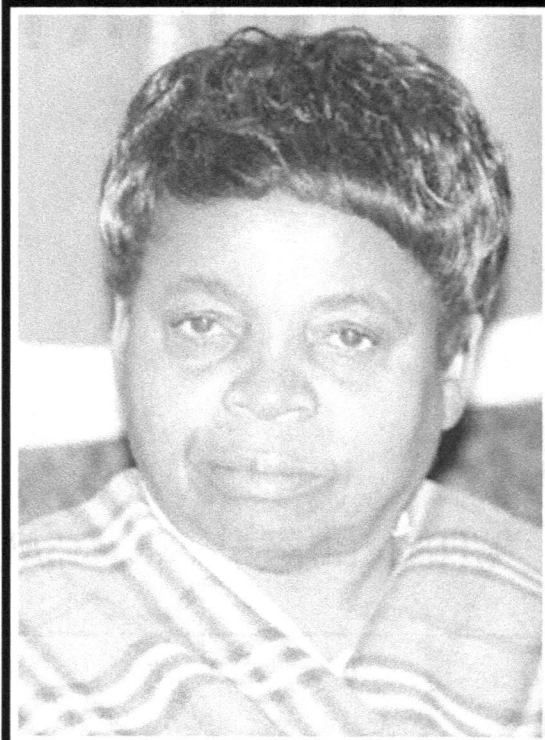

**CHIKAVA Betty
(ZANU PF - MP for
Mt Darwin East and
Member for Central
Committee)**

THE late Betty Chikava (nee Ndoro) started politics in 1960 in Highfields as a ZAPU youth activist and later joined ZANU under Ndabaningi Sithole in 1963. As a nurse she sourced food and medicine for freedom-fighters. She felt that women are still oppressed through gender roles which favour men and boys.

With little resources available, Chikava worked hard to develop her constituency. She sourced footballs for youths, linen for the hospital, books for schools, and various clothing through World Vision. Betty Chikava believes that through motivation and leadership workshops, women will become more involved in politics, and that for many women, joining politics becomes elusive because it involves vigorous campaigning and many days away from family.

She advocated for 50/50 gender representation at all leadership levels, and wants more young women to engage in politics because most of the women in current leadership positions are getting older, so there is need to groom younger females.

**CHIMBUDZI Alice
(Zanu-PF - Senator for
Mount Darwin and
Politburo Member)**

ALICE Chimbudzi has an interest in women and the girl child issues, and believes that emancipation of women comes through participation in decision making; hence women should attend meetings to air their grievances or get elected into local and central government positions

She started at cell level as chairwoman until she became a member of the Central Committee, Politburo and Senator in 2005. After attending the Beijing Women's Conference in 1995, she was inspired to launch the Girl-Child Program and mobilized female councilors and female teachers to sponsor two girls each from a primary school of their choice. Some of the girls later assumed leadership roles in teaching, police, and agriculture. She was chosen by people to represent her constituency as a senator. She was instrumental in increasing the number of female councilors to 14 seats out of 35 wards, the highest female representation at local government level in the rural areas.

Chimbudzi believes that all leaders should thrive to improve the well-being of the people they lead, and leads by example, for example, she ploughs the land for people in need in her Ward using her tractor; and that it is good to know how people you lead make a living.

NOTES

NOTES

NOTES

NOTES

**CHINOMONA Mabel
(ZANU PF - Former Deputy
Minister Home Affairs and
MP for Mutoko)**

MABEL Chinomona *(nom de guerre Memory Matimaitei)* joined the liberation struggle in 1975 at the age of 15. She is a survivor of the Chimoio massacre. After the war she trained as a secretary and became an MP for Mutoko in 1990. At primaries she faced resistance from traditional leaders who did not want a woman MP. In 1997 she became Deputy Minister for Home Affairs. Chinomona was instrumental in changing women police uniforms to include trousers, and going to Freedom Camp (Zambia) and Chimoio to rebury the war victims. She feels that leaders who start from grassroots level (bottom-up) understand people's issues and appeal to people. Mabel Chinomona worked with Plan International to provide fencing for schools and building classroom blocks and toilets.

She is using her allocation of money from the Constituency Development Fund to provide roofing for schools, providing grinding mills and generators in different wards. She is also assisting youth's groups and women to start a poultry project, providing pre-schools, toilets and electricity for clinics and painting schools and repairing some boreholes. Mabel believes that women MPs should be role models and lead by example. She feels that for many women leaders, if their partners/husbands are not supportive, the marriage can either end (divorce), or the woman can quit politics. She also wants women leaders to groom young people to take over, and for MPs to rise above partisan politics and stop heckling each other in Parliament at the expense of development. Leaders should appreciate diversity and different ideologies.

**CHITSA Enna
(MDC-T – Senator for
Masotsha Ndlovu)**

THE late Enna Chitsa started politics at a very young age when she joined ZAPU, but decided to leave politics when Zanu and Zapu forged a unity accord. She rejoined politics through the Trade Union, and was instrumental in the formation of the MDC. She realized that it would be very difficult for women to become MPs, because, "Men made sure that they did not give us a chance, they made it impossible for women to be MPs."

She decided to work for the party in a different capacity; as the National Vice President of the Women's Assembly, and in 2008 she was elected as Senator.

"When one is elected as an MP in an area, you are not just elected for your party but for the whole nation." It is this attitude that had seen Chitsa working well with her constituency as a Senator.

Enna Chitsa had two MPs in her constituency. She met with them and they took their discussions to the Lower House. She believed that women should be in politics because they are natural leaders although they are suppressed by society. Enna believed that political violence is not good for women, as it deters them from becoming involved. On 50/50 representation she believed it should be enforced by law. Although some husbands do not support their wives, Enna got support from her late husband, family and members of her church.

Dr Chung Fay (Former Deputy Minister of Administration for the Ministry of Education, and Minister of Education)

FAY Chung was born in 1942 to parents of Chinese heritage. Her grandparents came from the Canton Province of China in 1904. In Rhodesia even the Chinese children were segregated against at school "unless your parents were wealthy enough to send you overseas, or to South Africa, you couldn't enjoy primary and secondary education." she said in an interview with Ruth Weiss. Her aunt remained in the same class for five years because her parents were told "We don't allow any Chinese in this school." Going to school with Coloureds politicized Fay, because they were a rejected people by both the Africans and the Whites.

She found the colonial education for African children deplorable, and a symbol of oppression itself which only allowed one in five children to access secondary education. In 1973 Fay joined ZANU during the liberation struggles but was forced to exile in Tanzania and Mozambique. In 1980 she served as Deputy Minister of Administration for the Ministry of Education, and Minister of Education in 1988. Fay remains an active advocate for women's education, leadership and empowerment efforts in Africa. She has also co-founded the Forum for African Women Educationalists (FAWE), Women's University in Africa and Association for Strengthening Higher Education for Women in Africa (ASHEWA). In 2008 she campaigned as one of the members of the independent association of women suporting Mavambo political party for Presidency

MARCH

SUN	MON	TUES	WED	THUR	FRI	SAT

Dete Agnes (ZANU PF – Senator for Mazowe)

AGNES Angelina Dete has 4 MPs under her constituency. She supports the proposal for 50/50 representation, which she thinks will encourage female engagement in politics and decision making. 50/50 reflecting a zebra pattern, and will be beneficial to women especially as they will lobby for resources that benefit women, such as healthcare, maternity, water and sanitation, and that many women are dying needlessly in childbirth. Dete started politics in 1962 and supported the liberation struggle by providing food and clothes to freedom fighters. She was inspired to join politics by the oppression that black people especially women experienced under white minority rule. Women were not allowed to own Bank accounts or apply for ID cards.

Because of her history of working with women, they asked her to run for senate. Agnes was born in 1944 in Goromonzi where her parents worked on a farm.

Agnes Dete believes that many young women should be encouraged to join politics if they are educated on how it will benefit them and other women in general.

Dongo Margaret (Former MP of Harare East)

MARGARET (Mtetwa) Dongo was born in 1960, and joined the liberation struggle in Mozambique in 1975 where she was known as Tichaona Muhondo (nom-de-guerre). She is one of the survivors of the Chimoio massacres by the Rhodesian Security Forces. After independence she resumed her education (which she had aborted during the war); and later worked for Zimbabwe News Agency before becoming an MP for Harare East in 1990, she enlightened many woman in her constituency on political issues and encouraged and helped them to be economically independent. Margaret was instrumental for the formation of the Zimbabwe War Veterans Association in 1989 to campaign for the cause of war veterans who were destitute.

Margaret believes in gender empowerment and challenges all forms of gender oppression. She was the first female, to launch an opposition party, the Zimbabwe Union for Democrats, which is argued to have paved way for other opposition parties in the country. She believes in transparency, democracy and openness, and as an MP she was voted the parliament's most accessible member with a whopping 95 percent approval rating by the Mirror magazine.

In 2010 she won a Supreme ruling against a law which did not permit women to sign passport applications for their children. Only men were allowed to do so. Margaret does not believe in ministries of women's affairs to deal with women's issues, because *"women have problems in education, problems in finance, problems in all sectors so why should they say, 'Go to your own ministry! Fight your own battles and win?' This is divide and rule. This is what makes me take the position that I take because women suffered just the same as men in the camps and in the war".*

43

NOTES

NOTES

NOTES

NOTES

NOTES

DUBE-Gombami Gladys (MDC-T - Senator for Mabutweni Constituency)

WHILE most agree that women emancipation has been affected mostly by the way our society is structured under patriarchy. The late Gladys Dube felt that women themselves are not helping the situation and fuelling it by not working together to challenge gender disparities.

"When a woman is appointed to a position, she makes sure that she stays alone at the top and makes it impossible for other women to come there, maybe it is the way women were brought up that they want 'ukubukwa,' they want all men to look and admire them and that way they feel complete and if another woman comes along the attention will be divided."

She advises women to stop the mentality of thinking that they are flowers and have to be picked amongst all the other flowers. Gladys Dube believed when addressing political issues with men, women need not to be confrontational. It does not help the situation at all. She encourages women to engage men and to educate them. "When someone is confronted they build ammunition and it does not help our situation as women. Again it is those women who already are on top who cause this confusion so that they stay alone at the top."

At 47 year old Gombami, a mother of five children, wanted to find ways and work out strategies that can see women achieve 50/50 equal representation in Parliament. She believed that women should not remove ladders for other women when climbing the stairs, and should remember those women who have held the ladder for them to go up. "We can sing 50/50 as much as we want but if we do not change our thinking it will remain just a song," she said. Dube a mother of five died at the age of 47.

PROFESSOR Gaidzanwa Rudo
(Associate Professor of Sociology
at the University of Zimbabwe)

SHE ran as an independent candidate in the March 2008 election, and lost, but it was brave of her to run as an independent as a woman. She served as a Constitution Commissioner (1999-2000), and is on various boards and committees, including being a trustee of the Women's University in Africa. She teaches Social Policy and is a feminist human rights activist and a mother. Professor Gaidzanwa believes in women empowerment through education, and criticized the 2012 financial budget as it will do nothing to improve education for females.

"A salary-focused budget is not sustainable and that means there is not money for real education in 2012", said Gaidzanwa.

She also argues that although the $30 000 allocation towards gender mainstreaming for tertiary education is a welcome development in the 2012 budget, it does not match with the extent of gender imbalances existing in tertiary education, and that "Funding schemes should be structured with the purpose of strengthening female participation in technical and scientific sector higher education," she said.

Women like Professor Gaidzanwa are needed in parliament as they discuss real issues affecting women.

GOTO Rosemary
(ZANU PF – MP Hwedza
South Constituency)

ROSEMARY Goto, born in 1946, comes from Hwedza, Mashonaland East Province. She started politics during the war. She is a member of the Central Committee. She was a Senator for Chikomba-Hwedza (2005-2008), and is now MP for Hwedza South.

Goto sees lack of unity among women as the main obstacle to involvement in politics and decision making, and supports the positive role of WIPSU and NGOs in encouraging women participation through workshops. She supports the proposal for 50/50 representation and encourages women to support each other.

To challenge ageism Rosemary started an Athletics Tournament for people between the ages of 39 and 90 in her constituency which promotes physical health through sport, and both men and women participate. To support women in her constituency, Rosemary bought some grinding mills for different communities because women were travelling for long distances to grind their corn. She intends to start poultry project for women. She believes in projects that support sustainable development such as gardening and farming.

She would want to see more women going for culture exchange programmes to learn how other women are doing it. She herself went to Rwanda.

Notes

APRIL

SUN	MON	TUES	WED	THUR	FRI	SAT

HOLLAND Sekai (MDC – T - Minister of State for National Healing, Reconciliation and Integration in the office of Prime Minister)

SEKAI Holland is a founding member of the Movement for Democratic Change and has spent much of her time in Australia, and married an Australian husband.

Sekai's political activism began in the 1960s, when, together with her spouse Jim Holland, they formed Australia's Anti-Apartheid Movement and campaigned for Aboriginal rights. From 1973 to 1976 she was the Chairperson for Chimurenga General Council of Zanu (Pacific and Asia, Australia and New Zealand).

Hon Holland is a gender activist as well as political activist. She was also one of the founding members of the Zimbabwe Institute of mass Communication (ZIMCO). Holland is the MDC T Senator for Chizhanje, Harare province.

She is the MDC-T Minister of State for National Healing, Reconcilliation and Intergration in the office of Prime Minister.

KARENYI Lynette (MDC – T - MP Chimanimani West)

ELECTED MP for Chimanimani West in 2008, Lynnette Karenyi admits that it was not easy for her as a female politician from the oposition. She joined the MDC in 1999, and was elected councilor for Chikanga Phase 2 Ward 16, Mutare, in 2003. The council was suspended in 2005.

In 2006 she became the Provincial Secretary for Manicaland Province, and national organizing secretary for women. She feels that challenges faced by female politicians include inadequate resources to run successful campaigns, labeling, internal and inter-party violence.

She wants the government to reserve more constituencies for female parliamentarians to encourage women participation in politics, and feels that women are more empathetic to the needs of marginalized people.

NOTES

NOTES

62

NOTES

NOTES

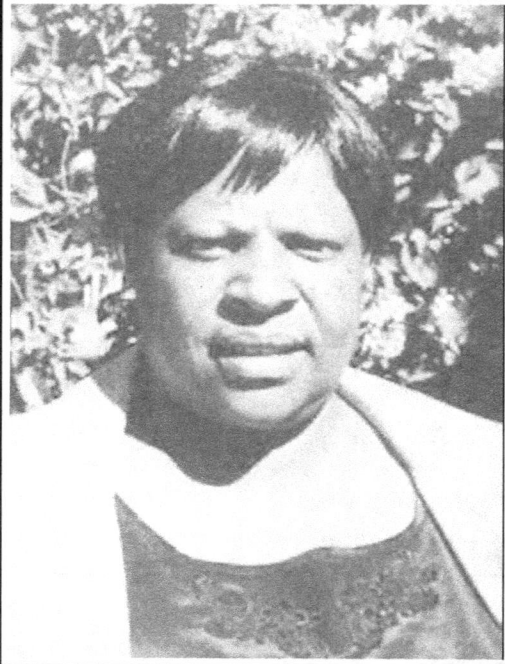

KATSANDE Aqilina
(ZANU PF – MP Mudzi West)

MOTHER of five, farmer, widow, and a politician! The late Aqilina Katsande felt that women were marginalized from occupying key decision-making positions in politics, yet women engage in community development projects that benefit women and children, and the few women who engage in politics get labeled as prostitutes or witches, she argued.

Born in 1960, Aqilina was elected MP for Mudzi East in 2005, beating her opponents with more than 8000 votes. She was also the Provincial Secretary for Women's League. As a female ward councilor and an MP, her major challenge was to fight cultural practices that oppress women and girls, such as marrying girl-children for food, or appeasing avenging spirits with virgin girls, both practices which were rife in her area.

**KATYAMAENZA Virginia
(ZANU PF - Senator for
Makonde)**

MOTHER of 6, Virginia Katyamaenza is the Senator for Makonde, which incorporates Chinhoyi, Mhangura and Makonde Constituencies. She started politics at a young age, and was elected deputy head girl in Standard 6. Although she was bright at school, her dream to train as a nurse was thwarted because her parents did not believe in educating girl children. She married a politician, who later participated at the Lancaster House Conference.

Virginia became a Chairwoman for a People's Movement in 1979; and Chairwoman for Chinhoyi District (1979-1984), and provincial Chairwoman in 1984. She is currently a member of the Central Committee.

Being a senator has boosted her confidence, and she wants more women to participate in politics and fight gender discrimination.

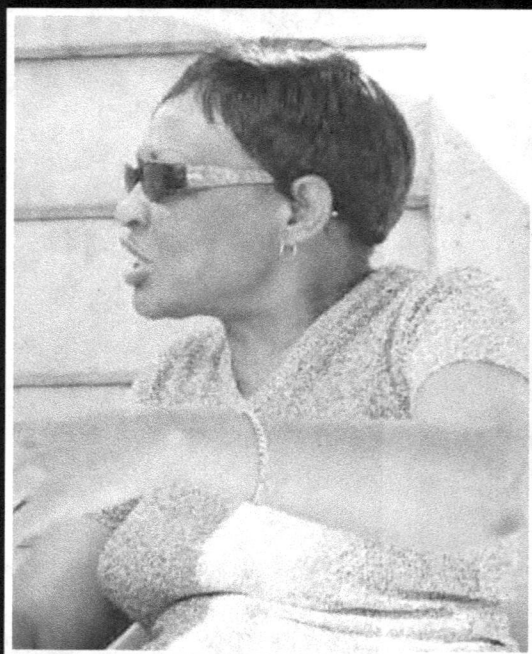

KHUMALO Tabitha (MDC-T – MP Bulawayo East)

TABITHA was theYouth Chair for ZAPU and joined the liberation struggle in Zambia and came back in 1980. She joined the Cold Storage Company Worker's Union and later ZCTU. Because she was the only woman in the Union, she was often referred to as a prostitute. She decided to join politics again because women who make 52% of the population are still marginalized and underrepresented in decision making positions. "There are issues that literally affect women which won't affect men", and gives the lack of sanitary wear which can cause many infections to women as an example. From 1999 to 2005 she launched a campaign known as Dignity Period, and in 2005 she sourced 40 tonnes of sanitary towels from the Director of Asian Society in Africa.

The government needs to pay more attention to women's health, including making it easy for women to access free health screenings (Pap smear, mammography etc) because women are dying in large numbers from breast cancer and cervical cancer.

Tabitha does not believe in the pull-her-down syndrome, but that those men as the major decision-makers in women's lives control the way women operate, and stigmatize women who participate in workshops especially those carried out in hotels. Women can achieve 50/50 representation if they unite because "As women we have the weapons of mass destruction, we are our own liberators, the onus is on us…"

MAY

SUN	MON	TUES	WED	THUR	FRI	SAT

**KHUPE Thokozani
(Deputy Prime Minister;
Vice-President of the Movement for
Democratic Change-Tsvangirai, MP
Makokoba)**

THOKOZANI Khupe the Deputy Prime Minister of Zimbabwe was born in Bulawayo in 1963. She worked for the National Railways, and through trade union, later became Secretary for the Zimbabwe Congress of Trade Unions Women's Advisory Council in 1991. She joined the MDC through trade union, becoming its Secretary for Transport and Logistics, and Member of Parliament for Makokoba in 2000. In 2009 she became the Deputy Prime Minister in the Government of National Unity (GNU), set upon the basis of the Global Political Agreement (GPA).

Thokozani Khupe is raising awareness on the sexual and reproductive health of women (the maternity issue) at the launch by CARMMA she said; "Zimbabwe Cares, no woman should die while giving life." Honourable Khupe was appointed CARMMA Goodwill Ambassador. She was also elected President for the United Nations Aids/Global Women Power Network.

She does not apologies for articulating women's rights, at the re-launch of 50/50 representation she encouraged women not to adopt the constitution if they are not well represented. "That constitution must have that provision which says that we need 50% representation of women in all decision-making bodies. It must be there and it must be very, very clear, we don't want any ambiguity, it must be very clear, over and above that we need a cabinet which will clearly state that any political party which does not comply, must be automatically disqualified from that election." She charged, and advised women to stop being crying babies.

"We constitute 52% of the population so there is no way we can continue crying, screaming and shouting that no we are not represented equally, no we are being short-changed, no ladies, let's do away with this victim mentality, let's do away with this cry baby mentality, let's stand up and stand on our two feet, let's start fighting for ourselves, we are many we can make it!"

MABHIZA Gladys (ZANU PF - Central Committee Member, Senator for Chikomba / Seke)

BORN in 1957 in Seke Village, Gladys Mabhiza is a symbol of the challenges faced by the girl child in a patriarchal society. She was educated by her father up to Grade 7 only, but determined as she was to get an education, she later attended night school at Seke 3 to get a decent education. She later worked for co-operative sewing uniforms, before becoming a security guard at Meikles Hotel and later worked at Greatermans shops for 18 years.

She joined the Commercial Workers' Union and was instrumental in fighting for a pay rise of 45% for all Greatermans workers. She left her job in 2003 to become a full time politician. She is a member of Zanu Pf Central Committee and Senator for Chikomba / Seke.

She empowers vulnerable women by giving them seeds such as Canoola to grow. Canoola is both a vegetable and an oil seed, and the women can squeeze the seeds to make vegetable oil. Seke, being devoid of natural vegetation, Gladys works closely with EMA to encourage sustainable environmental management in her constituency. Gladys believes in empowering women to be self-reliant as a way of tackling poverty. She believes women know the issues that affect households. Gladys also believe that women need to be united and strategize when it comes to working with men, who can easily de-campaign women.

"They know our power as women," she says.

NOTES

NOTES

NOTES

NOTES

NOTES

MADZONGWE Edna
(Senate President, Senator
for Chegutu and Member
of Zanu PF Politburo and
Central Committee)

EDNA Madzongwe is the first and only woman since independence in 1980 to hold the position of Deputy Speaker of Parliament. She was born in 1943 and grew up in a family of politicians, many who participated in the liberation struggle, which brought about independence in 1980. Although a committed ZANU PF member, Madzongwe says her strength as Deputy Speaker is her impartiality in her interaction with all MPs when she is handling parliamentary business or officiating at parliamentary functions.

Hon. Madzongwe is passionate about women's participation in politics and would like a situation where many women are actively involved in politics.

Mahofa Shuvai (ZANU PF - Former MP for Gutu South)

A SPIRITED and vociferous women rights activist, Shuvai Mahofa was appointed Deputy Minister of Youth, Gender and Employment Creation soon after the June 2000 parliamentary elections.

One of her goals she says, is to groom young women to become top leaders in political office.

She says her political vision now is to see women empowered and taking part in decision-making processes in national politics, including the civil service, commerce and industry.

"Women suffer more when there is poverty and this is the situation in my constituency today. This is further aggravated by the fact that they are the ones responsible for the children, the sick and the elderly," she adds.

She believes that women must be trained to join party politics from grass-root level so that they can compete at the same level with men. She says "Political parties are structured in such a way that is impossible for a woman to rise through ranks." According to the Standard Newspaper, many people tried to dislodge her political career, but enjoyed the backing of some people within the party including the late Vice-President Simon Muzenda. She earned the title "The Iron Lady" of Zanu PF politics.

She is a member of the Zanu PF's Women's League and she is in the Central Committee.

**MAHOKA Sarah
(ZANU PF - MP for Hurungwe
East Constituency).**

BORN in 1966 in a family of politicians, Sarah Mahoka joined politics to challenge the oppression of women. She supports the proposal for 50% female representation in parliament. As natural nation builders, women are approachable, empathetic, and should occupy more powerful positions in governance.

Women bear the brunt of bad decisions made my male dominated institutions, and its more women than men who die in road accidents as they go out to look for resources. There should be a separate budget for women's projects. More needs to be done to change laws that oppress women, and gender violence is perpetuated by low court fines, she argues.

Sarah has three children and grandchildren, and gets moral support from her husband.

Notes

JUNE

SUN	MON	TUES	WED	THUR	FRI	SAT

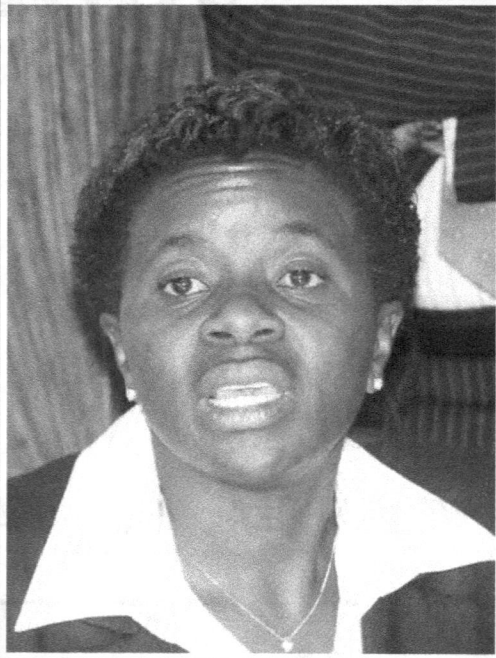

MAJOME Fungai Jessie (MDC-T MP for Harare West, Deputy Minister of Women's Affairs)

A LAWYER by profession, Jessie Majome was born in 1971. With her activism background, her understanding of the law, gender issues and her pursuit for justice, Majome's political career is destined for greater heights.

"I grew up in a politically charged environment, but I think the reason why I also got into it is because I had a kin sense of justice. I want all the time what is fair and what is just and you know I think it's just not right for anyone to do anything or hold down another person. I think it's the sense of justice that I've always have. I think that's the reason why I always speak out when things are unfair."

From an early age, Jessie Majome has challenged most of society's structures in her quest for justice, including challenging gender imbalances.

Majome encourages women to actively participate in the writing of the constitution no matter what political party they belong to. She believes that many women face financial drawbacks when it comes to funding their campaigns and projects when elected.

MAKONE Theresa (Co-Minister Home Affairs, and MDC-T Chairperson of the National Assembly of Women, MP Harare North)

THERESA MAKONE, the co-Minister of Home Affairs is a scientist, mother, businesswoman and politician. She became a political activist "way back in 1973 when I was a student at the University of Rhodesia in Mt Pleasant. I was arrested along with many other students for taking part in a strike over the arrest of student leaders and the racial discrimination in the allocation of residences at the campus."

After her release she absconded from university and fled to Botswana. In 1974 she enrolled at the University of Nottingham in the UK where she read for a Bachelor of Science degree in Bio-Chemistry and Food Science.

She later obtained a Diploma in Leadership Management from Waco University in Texas in the USA and another in International Therapy from the British Council of Aestheticienne When she returned home from the UK in 1978, she was the first female Development Chemist with a brewery company.

Three years later she moved to a pharmaceutical Company in Harare as a Quality Assurance Director before going back to the food industry as the first Chief Technologist, where two years later she was promoted to the post of Research and Development Manager.

Realizing that the company would never appoint her director because of her gender, she decided to resign to go into business. Minister Makone joined the MDC in January 2000 in Hwedza where her husband's family (Ian Makone) have a farm in Zviyambe small scale farming community.

"In 2006, I was elected unopposed by all the eleven district from Chivhu to Mtawatawa as the chairperson for the MDC in Mashonaland East," she said.

She assumed the post of chairperson of the MDC-T National Women's Assembly in October 2007. A mother of two daughters says she loves agriculture and runs a thriving poultry project at her rural home in Domboshava. John Gambanga

NOTES

NOTES

NOTES

NOTES

NOTES

Mandaba Maina Imelda (ZANU PF – Senator for Masvingo)

IMELDA Maina Mandaba became a Senator in 2008. To her it is very important to be involved in politics and decision making, especially since women understand issues that affect them and they can lobby for their enactment and implementation. Women are also patient when it comes to implementation and interpreting the laws to people. Laws regarding   maternity leave and pay should not be decided by men but women themselves.

People need to change their attitude and appreciate women's potential as leaders. As a nurse Imelda contributed towards the construction of the Matrimonial Causes Act, and she was aware of her rights when she decided to divorce her husband. Because many women do not understand the Act, she believes that they suffer in marriages because they are not aware that they too can initiate divorce proceedings.

Imelda is currently educating women on the proposal for the new constitution through COPAC. She is teaching women to start small businesses without borrowing loans, such as making candles and keeping bees for honey. Imelda urges all women to support each other, vote for each other because if they are divided, men take advantage.

Mangami Dorothy (ZANU PF – MP Gokwe)

DOROTHY Mangami started being active in politics in 1995. She is an MP for Zanu PF. Her main challenge is to balance the time between being with members of her constituency, Parliament and family.

She did not face major problems during her campaign apart from shortage of resources.

"I competed with a woman, my party decided that the position be reserved for a woman and only women competed in that constituency...it was not a tough thing as compared to when you are competing with a man with a lot of resources".

People applaud her because she consults them; and in one area the people requested the construction of a footbridge, because during the rainy season it becomes difficult for people to cross the river to go to the shopping centre and school.

Mangami feels that women should create space for themselves because no one will create space for anyone

Manyeruke Jenia (ZANU PF - Secretary for Muzarabani, Senator for Mash Central Province).

JENIA Manyeruke was born in 1952, in Chikomba, although her family moved to Muzarabani in 1966. She became the Political Commissar for ZANU in 1978, joined Women Action Group at independence and attended various leadership workshops, which heightened her gender awareness. Manyeruke became Senator in 2008, and did not face many challenges during primary elections because she had the support of women and youths. Some women discouraged her from competing (out of fear), but she felt the need to challenge men and represent women.

Although senators do not get financial help for projects, she makes follow-up when MPs in her constituency do some projects through CDF. She encourages more women to join politics because they will feel empowered and inspired. She wrote her O levels at the age of 58, and passed her driving license at the age of 54. She believes that gender and age should not be seen as barriers from achieving anything.

She wants WIPSU to carry out more workshops with women especially in rural and remote areas to encourage them to become active and get involved in decision making positions.

THE HISTORY OF WOMEN POLITICIANS IN ZIMBABWE

by
Joyce Jenje Makwenda

INTRODUCTION

AS WOMEN prepare for elections which may be held anytime from now, let us reflect on past elections and the history of women in politics in Zimbabwe.

The four-tire Zimbabwean election, which was mired by confusion and uncertainty, came and went. At a women conference in Beijing, China, 1995, it was recommended that 30% of any legislature should be women. Yet in Zimbabwe, unlike Rwanda where 49% of parliamentarians are women, the numbers of women parliamentarians remain very low.

In 2005 only 24 women were elected in the 150-member House of Assembly, constituting only 16% of the seats in the house. And yet it is the woman who wakes up every day confronted with problems of food for the children, clothes, income etc, a result of decisions made by men who dominate the law-making chambers. Women, by and large, remain accessories in the political arena largely dominated by men, yet they constitute more than 50% of the electorate. Their political activity largely remains confined to singing at rallies and campaigns, preparing the atmosphere for male speakers.

But what constitutes this failure for women to make meaningful inroads in politics? Domestic violence, intimidation, corruption, suppressed voices, controlled space, lack of economic empowerment, lack of encouragement and the stigma of sexism (onslaught on their sexuality) all contribute to gender imbalances in politics and mainstream decision making. Few women take the courage to participate as electoral candidates because of the fear of pre-election violence and intimidation.

However, despite the hurdles that women face in the political realm, they make do, and continue to strategies on how their voices can be heard in mainstream politics, as evidenced in the past historical eras in Zimbabwean political history, the most significant being the pre-colonial era; the Pioneer (colonial) era from 1890s; the Federation of Rhodesia and Nyasaland (1953-1963); the UDI era (1965-1979), and post-colonial era, which can itself be subdivided in various periods; 1980 to 1987, 1988 to 1999 from 2000 to 2008, and 2008- to today. Each era reflects a new woman involvement and participation in the evolution of Zimbabwean women political history.

It can never be doubted that in the pre-colonial Zimbabwe era, women's voices in politics were very strong. Mbuya Nehanda and Queen Lozikeyi are just but some of the examples.

PRE-COLONIAL ERA

The history of Zimbabwe can be traced as far back as 1400th century when the country was at the peak of its first phase of civilization and was thriving under the Monomotapa Kingdom. The reign of Monomotapa produced one of the most respected woman leaders in Southern Africa, Modjadji - the Rain Queen. In 1800 she left the Great Zimbabwe under controversial and mysterious circumstances and headed south to what is South Africa today to start her own Queen-dom. She founded a people known as the Balobedi who have been ruled by a Matrineal line of Queens. The fifth Queen Modjadji died in 2005 and has not yet been replaced. Modjadji is the forerunner of women's emancipation in Zimbabwe and the Southern African region.

In 1890 Zimbabwe was invaded by colonialists and the country was changed to Southern Rhodesia. In 1896 the Shona and the Ndebele revolted in what is known as the first Chimurenga. The first rebellion against British settlers was led by **Ambuya Nehanda**, a woman, through a spirit medium. Her legacy continued during the war leading to independence from White colonialists. Before she was hanged in 1898, she said, 'My bones will surely rise again!' Indeed, during the war of liberation ZANLA Forces were inspired and 'guided' by Mbuya Nehanda's spirit, which according to Ruth Weiss Nehanda's spirit had predicted that the war was going to be won by the black majority.

According to David Lan, Nehanda did not only inspire the struggle, but through art, her effigy became an important insignia of ZANU PF literature, with the effigy of her head and shoulders printed above that of Robert Mugabe. Today Nehanda's effigy is hardly used as it was during the struggle. What happened to Nehanda's painting?

To show the greatness of Ambuya Nehanda, on the eve of independence the newscaster played a song Mbuya Nehanda by the Zanu PF- Ideological Choir.

Similalry another version of the Mbuya Nehanda song became a hit when Zimbabwe got its independence and became almost like a national anthem of the country. The song was originally sung by the ZANLA forces to inspire them during the war. According to Margaret Dongo the song was composed by a female ZANLA cadre Muchazosiya Mabhunu who unfortunately died at Wampua Camp. The song was later re-arranged and fused with popular music by Virginia Sillah and the Harare Mambos band.

Queen Lozikeyi, King Lobengula's first wife, took over the reigns of the Ndebele nation in 1894 when the nation was in turmoil after King Lobengula's disappearance. Lozikeyi is argued to be one of the best political strategists in the history of Zimbabwean military history, making sure that the military was well equipped during the 1896 rebellion. She is argued to have led a better, well organized rebellion of 1896 than the 1893 rebellion (Marieke, Nyathi).

Like Nehanda, she too inspired the ZIPRA's war during the 1970s war. According to Jeremy Brickhill (ZIPRA Force), the ZIPRA fighters buried two bullets, one FN and one AK guns, at the queen's grave. The FN bullet represented the Rhodesian forces, while the AK bullet represented the guerrillas. The ZIPRA soldiers did this to inform Queen Lozikeyi's spirit that the country was at war and to ask her for strength. Maintaining a balance between political power and economic power, Lozikeyi is argued to have been

Queen Lozikeyi

one of the richest people in the history of Zimbabwe.

One cannot therefore doubt that Mbuya Nehanda and Queen Lozikeyi are the foremothers of Zimbabwe's liberation.

Zimbabwe managed to produce such powerful women because the role of a woman in the society was powerful during the pre-colonial era. During the pre-colonial days women's political position in society was very strong. It was strong in the sense that women participated actively in all spheres of society in Zimbabwe and the rest of Africa. They were women who were as chiefs and queens were very respected by their society. Besides holding the highest political position in society women had the control of the economy of their communities. Besides nurturing children and being the primary educator, they were also storytellers and would pass the history of the family to the new generation. In this context, women were custodians of the values of society and this gave them a much stronger voice.

Women also had the power to change the political system in the old traditional setting. By protesting naked they could remove the king/chief from power.

All the activities that women were engaged in during the pre-colonial era are closely intertwined with politics. Politics is about economic power, accessing information and disseminating it, the right to protest, and consciousness of cultural identity. Women played a pivotal role in these areas and this made their position stronger in society.

Colonial Era
The introduction of the colonialist systems saw the position of the African woman being weak in the society.

African women disappeared from almost all the structures that controlled the country and they became invisible in the history of the country.

White women were not significant either, partially because they were still very few of them in the colony. When white women became more visible in later years they were still regarded as second class citizens. This is how Doris Lessing interpreted the role of white women in colonial society: "The woman was not considered to be an equal to man. The White Rhodesian woman had to be pretty, a social asset to her man.... Their only power, indeed, lay in their control of household servants. Some women did enter the labour force but, for most part, their jobs - as secretaries, for example – merely extended their roles as the providers of services to men. Those who joined a profession were seen as odd."

White women did not enjoy the public space as their male counterparts and under this environment women could not even dream of being politicians. However, there were a few outstanding women like **Muriel Rosin** (1953), who made an impact across the racial divide and before her there was Tawse Jolly who was elected the first woman MP in Southern Rhodesia (1923). It was not until the 1950s and the 1960s that black women began participating in modern day politics. They realised that they could not continue to stand on the sidelines as they had to be involved in the running of their affairs which were controlled by politics.

Muriel Rosin

WOMEN AND POLITICS OF THE 1950s -1960s ....
AND BEING MARRIED TO THE STRUGGLE

In the 50s women got fed up with this situation and decided to take back their place in the society as decision-makers. One of the ways to get through to the oppressive government was to organize protest marches. Some of the women who were involved in early politics (1950s, 60s) were, **Ruth Chinamano**, **Sally Mugabe**, **Victoria Chitepo**, **Thenjiwe Lesabe**, **Julia Zvobgo**, **Mai Murape**, **Mai Nyamurova** and **Jane Ngwenya.**

Ruth Chinamano was the first woman political detainee at Gonakudzingwa, after leading a women's protest against colonial injustices against women by the government of the 50s. The authorities were not amused by the mob of women who had come to challenge them. "They would have loved to shoot us but they didn't, we were beaten by the dogs. Later on we addressed a meeting in Highfield of more than 30 000 and after that people went rioting. That is why they sent me to Gonakudzingwa detention." Said Ruth Chinamano in an interview in 1994.

Ruth participated in national politics during the federation of Rhodesia and Nyasaland, the UDI and post-colonial Zimbabwe. She put her country first before her children, who came second. In April 1964, Chinamano

Ruth Chinamano

was detained at Gonakudzingwa with her husband, Josiah Chinamano, the late Vice President Joseph Msika and Father Zimbabwe Joshua Nkomo. (They were the first four inmates at the prison) and she being the only woman. She and her husband were transferred to Hwahwa Prison where they remained until 1970. When they were released they were confined to an 8km radius restriction but were arrested again only to be released in 1974. Ruth Chinamano was reunited with her children after 10 years in 1975.

She held different posts in Zapu, and when Zimbabwe attained its independence in 1980, she held various posts in Zapu and Zanu PF and the government. She was one of the 8.6% of women elected to parliament on a PF ZAPU ticket from 1980-1985, she later became a member of the ZANU PF Central Committee member after the ZAPU and ZANU Unity Accord in 1987. She also continued to encourage women to take their place in the political arena and supported the electing of Joyce Mujuru as Vice President of the party and of the country.

In the 1950s a rare white woman Muriel Rosin was the only woman MP in the Federal government during the Federation of Rhodesia and Nyasaland. Muriel was known as the 'only man' in the Federal government. Muriel found it easy to mix with men at all levels. It was easy for her to interact with men because she had gone to a conventional school, which was very unusual in her days. In the interview that I had with her in the 90s, she said: "I think it was easier for me because I went to a conventional school, which was very unusual in my days so I got used to working with men. They respected me and they never ignored my ideas because I was just the same as them."

Rosin made meaningful contributions and was not intimidated when it came to discussions in the parliament. During her time, Muriel made tremendous changes in the Territorial government which was responsible for African affairs. Housing was a territorial matter and when Muriel was in the Territorial government she was very instrumental in building Highfield Township. She also convinced the then government to turn the Beatrice Cottages into a house ownership scheme which was an internal camp where the Germans had lived at the end of the war. Highfield and the Beatrice Cottages were the first to be under the home ownership scheme, whereas people living in other townships run by the City council signed a lease for 99 years.

Muriel also fought hard to try and have the Land Apportionment Act repealed, but unfortunately

Sally Mugabe

this was the weapon which the UDI used. During UDI she gave Smith a hard time. Smith had to send the secret service to her husband to try to refrain his wife, as they were scared to face Rosin.

While Muriel applauded today's women for fighting hard to attain high posts in politics she wished there could be more women in parliament.

Sally Mugabe is one of the women who became active in politics in the 1960s and she became the founding mother of the new nation of Zimbabwe in 1980. She was popularly known as Amai for the work she did for the country before and after independence.

She got married to Robert Mugabe in 1961, coming from an independent Ghana, Amai Sally was annoyed by open racial discrimination which was practiced in Rhodesia. Sally Mugabe demonstrated her political activism as early as 1962 when she was active in mobilizing women to challenge the constitution which resulted in her being charged with sedition and sentenced to five years imprisonment, part of which was suspended. In 1975 she joined her husband Robert Mugabe in Maputo, she found herself challenged to a new role of a mother figure to thousands of Zimbabwean refugees and revolutionaries. Her efforts in this role earned her the popular title Amai (Mother).

In the 1980s she founded the Zimbabwe Child Survival Movement. In 1981, she became the patron of Mutemwa Leprosy Centre in Mutoko and helped erase the social stigma associated with lepers. She also assumed patronage of many children's centres including disabled and orphaned children.

Amai Sally Mugabe also initiated projects aimed at rehabilitating prostitutes.

Joana Nkomo

She launched the Zimbabwe Women's Cooperative in the UK in 1986 and supported Akina Mama wa Africa, a London based African women's organization focusing on development and women's issues in Africa and the United Kingdom.

Amai Sally Mugabe died of a kidney aliment on January 27 1992 and became the first heroine to be buried at the National Heroes Acre.

Joana Nkomo (Mama Mafuyana), who married Joshua Nkomo (Father Zimbabwe) in 1949 was never to enjoy the physical company of her husband and accepting that she could lose or cede her husband to the struggle, made her a virtual widow. The couple was blessed with 4 children, with the husband's life fluctuating between long spells in detention and risky missions of the struggle, the burden of raising the family was hers. Single-handedly, she fended for the family ensuring that the children secured decent upbringing and decent education.

Her strength and resourcefulness as a mother released her husband from family chores giving him precious time to focus on leading and prosecuting the struggle. As she was married to the struggle, her motherly love was national as it went beyond her immediate family to embrace young cadres to and from various training camps and refugee centres.

At independence, up to her death, Mama Mafuyana worked for the unity of all Zimbabweans; mostly for the welfare of under-privileged children through the Child Survival and Development Foundation.

Her departure on the 3rd of June 2003 was a sad loss to the nation. She is buried at the national shrine. (ZBC Remembering Mama Mafuyana).

Julia Zvobgo was also very active in politics in the 1960s up to the time of her death. She was part of a demonstration in the 1960s and she was pregnant, dogs were set on the women who had demonstrated and beaten but the police did not touch her because she was pregnant.

Julia Zvobgo

In 1964 her husband Eddison Zvobgo was arrested and sent to prison, which became difficult for her as she had to raise children alone. In 1968 she decided to leave the country she went to the UK and then the United States. In 1977 she went to Mozambique during the height of the war, she came back in 1979 after the war and stood as an MP and she won, she was one of the few women MPs at independence. She is the third woman to be buried at the National Heroes Acre the National Shrine, not many women have been buried at the national shrine despite having fought the war just like their male counterparts.

The late **Sunny Ntombiyelanga Takawira** (Amai Takawira), a nurse by profession was married Leopold Takawira in 1955, who served as the Vice President of ZANU after supporting the(NDP) and later ZAPU. Amai Takawira was never to enjoy her marriage as her husband was either in prison or abroad fundraising and mapping out strategies for the party. After the arrest of Cde Leopold Takawira in 1964, she smuggled letters and information in and out of prison at Whawha, Gonarezhou and Sikombela Detention Centres as well as Salisbury Central Prison. They had three children which she was later to raise alone as her husband died mysteriously in prison in 1970.

Sunny Ntombiyelanga Takawira

According to Lindiwe Mimi Tsele who interviewed her in 1980; The death of her husband did not take away the resolve in Cde Sunny to work for the liberation of Zimbabwe. During her stint as a nursing sister at a clinic in Highfield near Mbizi Police Station, she contributed much to the liberation struggle through treating both civilians and those who were injured in the armed struggle.

She was also involved in the demonstrations organized by the nationalists' wives whose spouses were languishing in detention. They often demonstrated against discrimination of the colonial regime with women such as Ruth Chinamano which resulted in them being detained at Harare Central Police Station, only to be released after paying fines. Her home was also attacked in 1979 resulting in her two children, Gertrude and Leopold Jnr being injured. *(Interview conducted in 1980 by Lindiwe Mimi Tsele)*

IN 1980, Amai Sunny Takawira was appointed Senator for Midlands. After the ceasefire in 1980, along with her two sons, came many freedom fighters to stay with her at the family house in Highfield. She continued well into independent Zimbabwe providing shelter to many war veterans. She believed in leading by example. For instance, in the early 1980s, together with Tsitsi Munyati and many other women, Amai Takwira participated in sponsored walks and charity events. In 1980 she walked from Melfort to Harare Post Office to raise funds for wounded war veterans at Melfort.

Sunny Ntombiyelanga Takawira sadly died following complications arising from an operation of the womb at her Mt Pleasant home in Harare on the 13th of January 2010 and she is one of the few women at the National Hereos Acre.

THE 1970s .... THE LIBERATION STRUGGLE AND HOW WOMEN PARTICIPATED

The liberation struggle in the 1970s was fought in many ways; using the gun and by educating young Zimbabweans so that they could run Zimbabwe efficiently in different sectors. **Thenjiwe Lesabe** is one woman who had the welfare of young people at heart and in the 1970s, she organized scholarships for many to go and study abroad while she was in exile in Botswana. Many young people benefitted from the scholarships she organised.

Thenjiwe Lesabe's political career started in 1949 when she became an active member of a social club known as Gama Sigma Club in Bulawayo. The club was composed of intellectuals and others interested in social welfare matters including education for Africans in the country. The club acted as a think tank.

Thenjiwe Lesabe

In 1957 Lesabe was among the first people who joined the Southern Rhodesian African National Congress. She was among the first women to join the National Democratic Party (NDP) in 1960, Lesabe mobilised many people in Mzilikazi and Babourfields and formed a branch known as MZIBA (Mzilikazi/ Babourfields). She was the leader of the Zapu women's league, ZAWU, until the party was banned in 1962.

At the height of the clampdown on the leadership of the nationalist movement by the Ian Smith regime, In 1978 Lesabe went into exile. She helped send many young people to school all over the world and also helped with the training of exiles in camps.

When Zimbabwe attained its independence she became a Member of Parliament in Bulawayo and a member of the PF Zapu national executive. She was also national secretary of the Zanu-PF Women's League and a former Minister of National Affairs and Employment Creation. In 1990 she became Deputy Minister of Tourism before being elevated to Minister of Education, Sport and Culture. She was later appointed to the ministry of National Affairs and Employment Creation a post she held until she left the Government in 2000.

She was Member of Parliament for Umzingwane up to the 2000 elections. She quit Zanu PF in September 2009 and joined Dumiso Dabengwa in the revival of Zapu as a separate political party. The life of Thenjiwe Lesabe came to an end on Friday, February 11, 2011. Lesabe was buried at the family farm in Fort Rixon in Insiza district, Filabusi in Matabeleland South province.

In the 70s another white woman became a political activist and tried to correct the political imbalances through her work, she earned herself the title of *Ambuya Diana* (Grandmother Diana). **Diana Mitchell** fought hard to have some black children able to go to school and today she is an ambuya (grandmother) to many children whose parents she helped to educate during UDI, Black children and White children did not go to school together. One of the children she educated was John Indi who later became involved in theatre, film and he is an entrepreneur. The children of Black domestic workers in the affluent white areas were bused to schools in Black townships. In protest, Diana Mitchell, who was then Chairperson of the friends of African children, used to go door to door in

108

the affluent white areas raising money and clothes to educate Black children.

She used to ask the rich white residents: "How can you let these children live in your backyard, the most expensive areas of the country, and deny them schooling?" Diana Mitchell was for 15 years Press and Public Relations Officer for the Centre Party which fought Ian Smith's UDI.

"It was through this protest that I was groomed to be a politician." She said.

During the 1970s many women got involved in the liberations struggle to free their country from oppression, the liberation war saw both men and women taking up arms to fight colonial rule. Some of the women who joined the liberations struggle are **Jane Ngwenya, Eunice Sandi, Joice Mujuru. Oppah Muchinguri, Margaret Dongo, Freedom Nyamubaya, Monica Mutsvangwa** and many others.

Diana Mitchell

Although many women joined the struggle under ZANLA and ZIPRA, very few were rewarded after the war, when they were expected to assume the "woman's role". Reintegrating into the community was a double jeopardy. The society did not accept them as "women", and they found themselves working twice harder than the "ordinary" woman would do, so as to be accepted in the society.

Some lost themselves in the process and became more subservient than their counterparts who did not take up arms in the war. Many families would not approve of their son marrying an ex-combatant for a wife. Some of the women that I have spoken to find it very difficult to talk about their experiences both during and after the war, and sometimes wonder why they even went to war.

Jane Ngwenya, under the ZIPRA wing command, was one of the first women to take up arms and go into the bush to fight. She however regrets why she ever fought in the liberation war as no one seems to recognize the contributions she made and others of her time. Jane Ngwenya spent most of her years in politics, which saw her losing her marriage, as her husband became jealous that she was sometimes the only woman in a meeting full of men.

She also gave up her teaching career as she was outspoken about the way the teachers were paid compared to their white counterparts. She was to spend 9 years in confinement in Whawha and Gonakudzingwa Prisons.

"There are times when I regret why I ever fought for this country. Noone seems to remember or to recognize that sacrifice, the fact of the matter is we could not all become ministers but the political set-up is all wrong." Said Jane Ngwenya in an interview with Nelson Chenga –Herald.

Ngwenya joined the African National Congress in 1959. The following year she became a national council member of National Democratic Party. The NDP was banned on December 9, 1961 and ZAPU was launched 10 days later, with just about the same leadership. Ngwenya was appointed national secretary for women's affairs.

Jane Ngwenya

Between 1964 and 1971 she was detained at the notorious

Whawha and Gonakudzingwa. Her appetite for fighting white rule grew even stronger while in detention. At Whawha she was thrown into solitary confinement as punishment for inciting other women prisoners to challenge poor conditions in jail. She said wet and cold conditions in jail resulted in her developing arthritis that has now worsened with age.

She escaped to Zambia where she was based in Lusaka under the Zimbabwe African People's Union and was responsible for the welfare of freedom fighters in operational zones. While in Lusaka she was seriously burned in a parcel bomb blast that killed the Zapu military leader Jason 'Ziyapapa' Moyo on January 22 1977. She was elected to Parliament on PF- Zapu ticket in 1980, representing Matabeleland North.

As one among the many women, who participated in the war of liberation, Ngwenya is concerned that deeply ingrained tradition still affects the rights of women in general. "The Government is trying to recognize us, not that it likes us, but because we fought to be recognized", she said. *(Nelson Chenga – The Herald – June 10, 1999).*

Joyce Mujuru is one of the few women who was in the liberation struggle who is holding a high post in the government. In 1973, Joice Mujuru left the country to join the liberation struggle, where she showed leadership qualities and rose through the ranks of Zanla, the armed wing of Zanu (PF).

She became medical assistant, then military commander and Central Committee member. She has held different posts since independence in 1980. After independence women were appointed as ministers, although very few got full ministerial positions, she was Minister of Youth, Sports and Recreation. Most of them assumed positions of deputies. Some of the women were **Naomi Nhiwatiwa** and **Victoria Chitepo** who was the Deputy Minister of Education and Culture and Naomi Nhiwatiwa became Deputy Minister of Post and Telecommunications.

Joyce Mujuru *(nom de guerre Teurai Ropa)* was one of the few women who were appointed as full ministers.

As a Minister of Women Affairs, she lobbied for the Legal Majority Act 1992, which opened doors for women to be able to take decisions without men. Joice Mujuru continued to encourage women to fight for their rights, and also encouraged them to join trade unions. She remains the highest ranking woman in Zimbabwe politics, the first woman to attain a high post in government as the vice president of the country. Joice Mujuru was the Minister of Community Development and Women's Affairs at the attainment of Zimbabwe's independence in 1980.

At a Women's Day rally on March 8, 1983, Joice Mujuru also known by her Chimurenga name Teurai Ropa Nhongo, urged women to press for their rights.

She told the meeting that the goal of Zimbabwe as a developing socialist state was equality for all citizens before the law.

Naomi Nhiwatiwa

Victoria Chitepo

She said, "Women participated in the national liberation struggle for human rights, and their resources must be made full use of in a mutually complementary manner, rather than in a master-servant relationship, which smacks of exploitation of one group by the other?"

On that same occasion, she urged women to join trade unions. Women, she said, could do as well as men if they were only given the chance.

But she pointed out that in Harare out of 86 councillors, only two were women, and Bulawayo had none. In Parliament, the body that represents the whole society, there were only 12 women out of 140.

She pointed out, too, that although the Government was the largest employer of labour, no woman yet sat on the Public Services Commission.

"These are the areas we need to transform," she said. (Weiss 1986, 23)

The demands for women's rights from almost all quarters of society including the highest echelons were growing.

Joice Mujuru held different posts in Government before she became Vice President on December 6 2004.

In 1985 she became Minister of State up to 1988. She then became Minister of Community Development, Cooperatives and Women's Affairs up to 1992.

She was Governor and Resident Minister of Mashonaland Central Province up to 1996.

She also served as the Minister of Information, Posts and Telecommunications for a year, and in 1997 she was assigned Minister of Rural Resources and Water Development up to 2004 when she was appointed Vice President.

One woman ex-combatant who changed the terrain of post-independence Zimbabwean politics is **Margaret Dongo** *(nom de guerre Tichaona Muhondo)*. She refused to give up her fighting spirit, she became the first ever woman independent MP standing for Sunningdale. She served as a parliamentarian for many years later founding the Zimbabwe Union for Democrats, the only political party headed by a female.

Believing in women economic empowerment, Margaret Dongo engineered a lot of self-help projects for women during her tenure as a member of parliament for Sunningdale. She educated people in her constituency on their rights and her constituency Harare South was dubbed the 'Republic'. She explained the calibre of women in her constituency in an interview I had with her in the 90s.

"Women in my constituency are quite different from women of other constituencies. They are not the so-called intellectuals or academics who at times don't even know their rights, despite the fact that they are in advantageous positions. Some women in my constituency have never gone to school. But when they stand up to tell you their rights, their role as women, and their role as citizens of Zimbabwe, you feel proud."

She has not been afraid to challenge structures particularly those which oppress women and children. Recently in 2010 she challenged the traditional set up regarding inheritance. The rural areas sometimes makes it difficult for women to voice their concerns as regards inheritance, to traditional law the home belong to the males of the family. A woman was chased away from her home in Mhondoro rural by her in-laws, after her husband and son had died, Margaret intervened and she was brought back to her village.

Margaret Dongo has been a trailblazer in many ways she co-founded together with a few other freedom fighters, the National Liberation War Veterans Association, designed to champion the cause of demobilized ex-combatants who had become destitute. In 1990, Dongo was elected a

ZANU-PF member of parliament. She quickly pushed for a war veteran's administration bill.

Because of her being vocal in Parliament, Margaret Dongo fought single-handedly to stop some bills from becoming law. At one time a male parliamentarian threatened to beat her up when he felt challenged.

Attempting to retain her seat in the 2000 election, Dongo's house was attacked by a group of 60 opponents who threw rocks through the windows. She lost the elections, but continues to fight for women rights single-handedly. Now based in Mhondoro, she continues with her activism work and she has helped a number of people particularly women to understand their rights.

WOMEN AND EQUAL REPRESENTATION IN PARLIAMENT; PROBLEMS, STRATEGIES,...

Oppah Muchinguri feels that although Zimbabwe has almost 19 pieces of legislation in favour of women, more needs to be done in terms of implementation, including allocation of land to women, where 16% only of the land has been distributed to women. She prides in the role played by women during the liberation war "I am a politburo member, but I'm also a war veteran who fought side by side with men...Women's emancipation did not just come without a price. We went through the war of liberation where we lost sons and daughters of Zimbabwe...

It was not the easiest thing for us women in Zimbabwe..." she said, at a 50/50 representation work-shop held in Harare on 3 August 2011. She believes that women participation in decision making is the key to women's development. "We have witnessed countries like South Africa performing so well to ensure that there are more women in decision-making. Same for Mozambique, and other countries...we have now decided as women of Zimbabwe that we need to speak with one voice." She continued.

Oppah feels that although Zimbabwe has almost 19 pieces of legislation in favour of women, more needs to be done in terms of implementation, including allocation of land to women, where 16% only of the land has been distributed to women. Muchinguri believes that economic empower-ment for women will only be achieved if women stand up and fight for gender balance; including increased participation in the educational system, political decision making workforce, and the more women become economically independent the less they are likely to remain living in difficult situations in their families, discriminatory workplaces and in unhappy marriages.

"There has to be a logic noise out there or else we will lose it, already men are saying, this is wrong, 50/50 is too much, we should not reserve seats for women, they have already looked at their space, that they may not come back to Parliament, so how do we as women join hands to make sure that we insist that what comes from the people must see the day. We need to wise up so that by the end of the day we don't lose the 52% voices out there." Said Oppah Muchinguri who is lobbying for 50/50 representation of women in parliament.

Oppah held many portfolios after independence. She was the Private Secretary to the President from 1980-81; Deputy Minister of State for External Affairs from 1989-93; and Minister of Wom-en's Affairs, Gender and Community Development from 2005 to 2009 among other portfolios. She is the Secretary for the Women's League in Zanu PF, she is also a politburo member, the highest policy-making organ in Zanu PF.

While women are doing everything they can in order to be in the mainstream politics, they are faced with stumbling blocks which makes it impossible for them to attain the highest decision mak-ing body in the country. Amongst other obstacles political violence plays a major role in blocking women's participation in politics.

Due to pre-election political violence, women sometimes drop out of the race for political office; **Betty Mutero** has dropped out of the race twice. Mutero, the first black councillor in Bulawayo's

Njube Township in the 50s, was active in women's clubs and came into politics through her community work has always been interested in council politics in order to help her community. While in Bulawayo in Njube, Betty Mutero helped in the building of the African Children's Helping Hand Crèche, which still stands to this day. Because of her commitment to her community Betty Mutero was elected a Councillor for Njube, beating all the men who had contested. After independence she worked with the Ministry of Women's Affairs. Since then she has been based in Harare and continues to be active in community issues.

Women's clubs played a very important role in uplifting women's lives in the 50s, 60s, 70s and as a result some women became politically conscious through these organizations. Some of the women who were active in women's clubs besides **Betty Mutero** are **Helen Mangwende**, **Tsitsi Munyati** and **Mai Mutsvairo**. Even today many women have been politically concsientised through working with their communities, because of responding to the

Betty Mutero

needs of their communities they have ended up in parliament as the communities feel they are the right people to represent them in parliament. Some of the women who have worked with their communities and are now in parliament are **Sithembiso Nyoni, Elina Shirichena, Jenia Manyeruke, Gladys Mabhiza**, and many others.

In 2000, Betty Mutero dropped out of the parliamentary election race in order to protect her dignity. "I don't want to end up running in the township lifting my dress or without a dress at all [naked], because of violence, I want to keep my dignity," she said. She saw how some male politicians used money to buy votes by taking advantage of the desperate situations of women in the townships, and also buying beer for the youths who would in turn become violent and attack political opponents. Betty, who was a ZANU PF candidate, said she could not corrupt and turn the youths into hooligans by buying them beer, the very same people that she would like to lead, so she decided she would watch the race from a distant.

Betty Mutero feels that after independence many women were diverted from participating in active politics because of the excitement which was brought by the independence. "Now they have realised that there is none who can articulate their problems for them in parliament except them-

selves." Although women are fighting to have a bigger representation in parliament, people still need a lot of civic education to realise how important it is to have women in parliament. Betty Mutero feels today's campaign has become too complicated and expensive, which is a stumbling block for many women.

The late **Mavis Chidzonga** a ZANU PF candidate and MP for Mhondoro (1995-2000), was a victim of violence, she said that the violence starts in parliament where women are intimidated, humiliated and silenced, sometimes the whole saga turning to physical abuse when the male politicians feel challenged by women. Mavis explained her experience in parliament.

"To survive in that environment one has to either just give in and sit back and not take part in a number of activities then you are a good girl, then you are alright. Males feel threatened by your presence or if you happen to bring out according to them anything that is intellectually threatening. For example on my part the first time that I spoke in parliament, I responded to the President's speech and I seconded the motion made by Houn-

Mavis Chidzonga

ourable Mataure, eh phones rang that evening throughout Harare. Men were phoning each other saying have you seen this new breed which has come from Mashonaland West ? There was already fear that I was a threat to some men and I didn't realise it, they were phoning each other saying this should not come from a woman."

Working with the grassroots made it easy for Mavis to know how to respond to issues that were being discussed.

"I had researched my response, I had brought the issue from the grassroots, I had gone through my constituency so even though it was my three weeks of parliament I had gotten enough information about the whole of my constituency. I brought in well researched issues and real issues that were coming from the people, this apparently had happened rarely, most of the speeches were mediocre type of speeches. I was commended by the speaker that it's one of the speeches that we have had in the last parliament, that it is very good. When it was lunchtime they were comments, you know things like its coming from a woman, who wrote the speech for you it must have been a man you know it's just too good to have been written by a woman."

The abuse of women in parliament can turn into violence if some male parliamentarians feel challenged. Mavis gave a very interesting example regards violence perpetrated to women parliamentarians.

"I would actually like to take it to a smaller level for example in a house, in a family if you find a man beating up his wife it is a sign of weakness, not for the woman but for the man who decides that the only way to convince or to control the woman is by beating her up. The issue here is he can't discuss issues with the woman, he can't if the woman is strong enough to want to communicate with the husband if he can't handle her intelligence then he resorts to violence. So I see this as a method used by politicians, if they can't handle their opponent male or female they resort to violence because they think if we put fear in this person and their supporters, then we will win the election but that's not the good method of winning elections. People should be able to be free to campaign, free to challenge each other on the platform and bring out real issues that matter to the people, that would actually help a developing country like ours not to resort to forcing people. You might force them into the ballot box but you are not solving the problems of the country."

Mavis Chidzonga lost the 2000 elections by a small margin, she was running on a Zanu PF ticket. She was hurt by loosing because she had some projects going with The Children of Mhondoro in building the road to Mhondoro.

She felt male and females in Zimbabwe are not ready to have female leaders, "You can't change people's minds who have had scuds and scuds of beer for months or presents of machines from male counterparts." She charged.

Mavis passed away in 2011.

Priscilla Misihairabwi-Mushonga, an outspoken MDC T, parliamentarian (2000-2008) (2008- [MDC N]) spoke of some of the problems she encountered when campaigning in 2000.

"I ran into a police station for sanctuary when some rowdy youths wanted to beat me, only to be told that I could not stay in the police station as the station would be stoned!"

Priscilla discouraged violence no matter what and encouraged an atmosphere which will encourage people to vote freely, "Unfortunately the people that bore the brunt of that violence were women... either in actually being physically beaten but because women have problem reporting even to the status quo, or being able to expose themselves to the media their stories went unreported, the same thing with cases of rape, a lot of sexual abuse happening and we know how it is with sexual abuse and women coming out and saying you know I've been sexually abused not many

114

women can actually do that"

Despite the problems that she faced during campaigning she was elected MP for Glen Norah in 2000.

During her time as Glen Norah's MP, she also served as the shadow foreign minister for the Movement for Democratic Change. When the party split in 2005, she remained with the MDC formation, and was elected Deputy Secretary-General of that party. She has been representing her party in the Zimbabwean political negotiations.

In 2009 she was appointed Minister of Regional Integration and International Cooperation, in the government of national unity in the 2011 MDC congress she was elected the party' Secretary General a position she will hold up to the next congress in 2016. She is the MDC chief representative at JOMIC (Joint Monitoring and Implementation Committee) and COPAC the Constitutional Parliamentary Committee a committee in charge of writing the Zimbabwean constitution. Priscilla is a champion for women's rights, and is the only female negotiator in the GPA (Global Political Agreement).

During the same year (2000) **Thokozani Khupe**, a former trade unionist and Deputy President of MDC Tsvangirai, now Deputy Prime minister of Zimbabwe was also attacked while campaigning. A trade unionist, Thokozani Khupe became Deputy Prime Minister of Zimbabwe in 2009. Her political history is entrenched in the Labour Movement.

Could she have heeded to the call by then Minister of Community Development and Women's Affairs, Joice Mujuru who encouraged women to join trade unions in 1983?

Thokozani Khupe served in the Zimbabwe Amalgamated Railway Union (ZARU) in 1987.

In 1991 she was elected Secretary for the ZCTU Women's Advisory Council and also a General Council member of the ZCTU. In 1999 she participated in the formation of the Movement for Democratic Change party, in which she was elected as a National Executive member responsible for Transport, Logistics and Welfare.

In June 2000, she was elected Member of Parliament for Makokoba Constituency in Bulawayo. Thokozani Khupe has been the Deputy Prime Minister of the Government of National Unity since February 11, 2009.

She is also the Vice President of the Movement for Democratic Change (MDC-T) whom she represents in Parliament.

She does not apologies for articulating women's rights, at the re-launch of 50/50 representation she encouraged women not adopt the constitution if they are not well represented. "That constitution must have that provision which says that we need 50% representation of women in all decision-making bodies. It must be there and it must be very, very clear, we don't want any ambiguity, it must be very clear, over and above that we need a cabinet which will clearly state that any political party which does not comply, must be automatically disqualified from that election." She charged, and advised women to stop being crying babies.

"We constitute 52% of the population so there is no way we can continue crying, screaming and shouting that no we are not represented equally, no we are being short-changed, no ladies, let's do away with this victim mentality, let's do away with this cry baby mentality, let's stand up and stand on our two feet, let's start fighting for ourselves, we are many we can make it!"

STRATEGIES AND SOLUTIONS

While violence has been cited as a stumbling block for women to achieving their dreams as leaders in politics **Monica Mutsvangwa** says that, it is only women themselves who will change this. She advices women to educate men and help to take away the fear in men which has to do with seeing women as mothers and they are scared that once they are in parliament they will 'control' them.

Men feel that the space in the home is controlled by women so they have made sure that the space outside the home is theirs and will make sure that they keep it away from women.

"In their lives they started off under mum, mums doing everything for them, mum telling them stop that, so women have always been too strong for them. And then they get into marriage, they have a wife, women are very strong in marriages. In my own culture where I come from, the Samanyikas', the women *vanototonga, muri mumusha chaimo hapana zvirango zvinoitwa anamai vedu vasipo,* (Women are in powerful positions in the family in the Manyika tribe) so again, for man, politics is something , they want to make it their own space." Mutsvangwa explains further.

"They look at women and they see that they are too strong and they come again to the political ground, then they really don't have any space anymore but look it's about educating men. It's about educating them. Let's take the fears out of them that once the woman is around me she is going to act like a mum to me, because as women it's natural we micro, I don't want to call it micromanage but as women we go into detail."

According to the Young Women Christian Association (YWCA), Zimbabwe elected 28 women into its Lower House of Assembly in their March 29 (2008) general elections. Yet the election saw a 49% increase in women candidates since the last election of 2002. A total of 919 women contested for seats in what is proving to have been a landmark election.

In Zimbabwe women continue to fight to be in mainstream politics. **Sarudzayi Chifamba-Barnes** a Gender and Political Activist encourages more education, a free and fair campaigning arena as well as introducing a gender quota system for the selection of parliamentarians in the constitution which could help increase women involvement in politics.

Countries where quotas for women have been written into the constitution or introduced through national legislation include Rwanda, Uganda, Argentina where it is mandatory that 30 per cent of elective posts be reserved for women, and India where 33 percent of the seats in local municipal bodies are reserved for women. Denmark, Norway and Sweden ¬ are among the countries with the highest political representation of women in the world. Sweden has 40% of parliamentarians as women, while Finland has 34 %, Norway has 38%, Denmark has 34% and Iceland with 25%. In the UK the New Labour Party introduced gender quotas for selection of parliamentarians, and in 2005 New Labour Party had 98 women members of parliament out of 258 compared to 17 out of 180 for the Conservatives. It is arguable that women can change policy agenda, as they can lobby for higher priority to social policy issues like education, health and pensions as opposed to higher budgets for defence.

Women in Zimbabwe have tried to get into politics through the women's wings in their political parties, (Women's League – Zanu PF and Women's Assembly – MDC), but some feel most women become too comfortable in the women's league and fail to penetrate the main structures. While the women's wing is good for development, **Eunice Sandi** a veteran politician encourages women that it should not keep them away from the male domain especially during elections.

"You are there, you are fixed up, at a corner somewhere doing your own thing as women, you don't see the other side, you don't even want to, that's why we are still challenging each other so much and because of that we are not getting there." She advices. "I believe we should focus with the agenda of promoting women in the manner that it should be, the manner is don't challenge a

116

woman who is already in a position, get the positions that the men are holding so that you become more in the set-up. What is the point of having 10 women out of 160 men, it does not work, then you go there and you fight for those 10 posts."

Her sentiments were echoed by **Lucia Matibenga** who has spent most of her time fighting for women's rights. Her activism started in the labour movement, she is now the Minister of Public Service.

"I can tell you that in politics things are still difficult for us women, because of women's wing groups, it is as if we should be fighting from our corner as women, we seem to be conditioned to fight for mafufu (crumbs). What we should do as women is to use the women's wings in our parties as factories to push women in the main wing, we should make sure that once we have a woman in the main wing we do everything in our power to have her stay there." She continued to explain, "You see, and the women are beginning to talk about that in the women's caucus of Parliament for example, but I am also saying that the women themselves need to interrogate their own organizations and say women's league, what role do we want it to play in the party? Is it just auxiliary? Are we going to the main? Or also in the main of playing main politics and how are we going to do that? Because parties like the ANC, Zanu PF, and ZAPU, have had women's wings since 1963 but those names we used to hear when we were young in the women's league have not yet graduated to be in the main, the likes of Shuvai Mahofa. Do you mean that *madhonofisi* (a lock which is not removed from the door), which do not grow up, because I would want us to fix that. Whenever we have a women's wing congress we should make sure that we remove the whole top leadership and have it in the mainstream, and have new women. It is time to transform those women's assemblies of this world." She charged.

The Women's Caucus Group is bringing together women from different political parties to try and address the problem that women are facing as they try to chart their way into the political arena.

The aim of establishing a Women's Parliamentary Caucus was for women parliamentarians to rise above party politics and address issues of common concern as women.

The Zimbabwe Women's Parliamentary Caucus was launched in October 2001 in response to the SADC Parliamentary Forum initiative with the assistance of AWEPA (Association of European Parliamentarians for Africa.

The operations of the Caucus are guided by a Constitution which provides for, among other things, membership and management of the Caucus

Membership to the Caucus is open to all Zimbabwean Women Members of Parliament and Associate Members, upon payment of a prescribed fee.

An Associate Member is any former woman Member of the Parliament of Zimbabwe.

However, Associate Members are not entitled to take part in the management of the Caucus and cannot vote.

The current composition of the Management Committee is as follows:
a)   Chairperson - Hon. B. Nyamupinga (ZANU PF)
b)   Vice Chairperson - Hon. K. Chabuka (MDC-T)
c)   Secretary - Hon. S. Ncube (MDC-T)
d)   Vice Secretary - Hon. A. Ndhlovu (ZANU PF)
e)   Treasurer - Hon. B. Chikava (ZANU PF)
f)   Committee Members – Hon M. N. Mandaba (ZANU PF);
        Hon. A. Muloyi Sibanda (MDC-T); and
g)   Ex-Officio Members - Hon. O Muchena (ZANU PF), Hon. N.M. Khumalo (MDC),
        Hon. M. Matienga (MDC-T), Hon.
h)   Patron of the Caucas – Hon. E. Madzongwe (ZANU PF) (President of the Senate).
i)   The Director Research, Mrs. Christine Mafoko, assisted by Ms. Farai Hondonga provides
        the administrative secretariat of the Caucus.

Since its inception in 2001, the Caucus has achieved some of the following in line with its objectives and Plan of Action, the; Sexual Offences Bill, Constitution of Zimbabwe Amendment No. 17 Bill, Domestic Violence Bill and Gender Mainstreaming in Legislation Objectives

Angeline Makwavarara

It is not only in parliament that women are spearheading the political agenda for women's emancipation and the 50/50 representation in politics but across the board. It is only when women are in every structure of the society's decision making that they will be a feeder system to the main political structures from grassroots to – parliament. Since the 1980s when Zimbabwe attained independence women have held posts as permanent secretaries, ambassadors, etc. **Angeline Makwavarara** was the first woman permanent secretary and she was also the first female ambassador at independence. Makwavarara also opened those closed door in other fields; she was the first print journalist and the first black Nursing Tutor.

Some of the women who have followed in her footsteps as ambassadors are; **Amina Hughes** who was ambassador in Sweden, **Trudy Stevenson** in Senegal, **Chipo Zindoga** in Namibia, **Jacquiline Zwambila** ambassador to Australia, **Thandiwe Dumbutshena** in Malawi and **Hilda Suka Mafudze** in Sudan.

In the constitution making we have seen women also taking influential positions amongst them –

Oppah Muchinguri, Monica Mutsvangwa and **Jessey Majome.** It is through the constitution that women will decide how their lives are going to be run. Monica Mutsvangwa is part of the 25 select Committee Members who are spearheading COPAC, and she is the co-Vice Chair. She is also Deputy Minister for Women's Affairs and she is the Chairperson of Information and Publicity for COPAC. It is through COPAC, that she is pushing for equal representation of women in government.

The constitutional public arena is the most important arena for making advances and for changing, turning around and undoing this harm that the society has been doing to women. While it has been a challenge bringing to the fore issues of gender balance, Majome

Amina Hughes

will not tire discussing issues to do with the emancipation of women and equal opportunities.

Majome wishes to see super structures corrected, and the laws that regulate our country in the constitution, if this is not done women will not realize the fruits of other wonderful things that they are doing across the board. She encourages women to demand equality.

"So in the outreach you would find that women were the majority of participants in this exercise, at least physically they were present, they were there, their bodies were right there, they came out in their numbers and they outnumbered men and the good thing is that from those meetings they came out a very clear call for 50/50, it was clear women want equality in the constitution and what's left now is then for those demands to be reduced to writing so that we have constitutional guarantee of equality between men and women and an end to discrimination right through the constitution."

Majome also sites economical challenges that women face as a drawback, as they fail to fund their campaigns and projects when elected. Whereas men are sounder economically and the fact that they are the Captains of Industry they have an advantage over women as they network easily with their male counterparts. While they are women who are also influential in industry they are not as many as man.

"We need to start engaging in dialogue with women in industry so that they understand the need to do networks and also support women in politics because as a woman If I am going to be knocking on the doors of the Captains of Industry, I might not be understood, because unfortunately we have a long way to go also in having women's sexuality taken out of politics, because of sometimes how people relate to us." Jessie Majome explained.

While economic challenges have been cited as a drawback for women politicians particularly when they are campaigning, **Sithembiso Nyoni** encourages women to use human and social capital in order to be able to campaign and be involved in politics. Nyoni advices women to look for resources around them, what they have in their midst and use that to help them when campaigning.

"Make sure you have the resources. Do you have a car? If you don't have make sure you have human resources, the social habitants, either have capital or social capital, people will help you." She goes on to explain social capital.

"I have social capital as well and my biggest social capital is my family, I have a good husband, I have good children, I have a good family who understand me, who support me, that is very important."

CONCLUSION

Patricia Ndlovu the only woman councillor in Beitbridge feels it is important for a woman to be in politics, she says, "Everything that we do is politics, even if we may choose not to believe it. Wherever you walk its politics! The water that you drink is politics!" Said Patricia Ndlovu, the only woman councillor in Beitbridge, who feels why it is important for women to be in politics as councillors and parliamentarians. She would like to encourage men to support their wives to be in politics, as women politicians are working towards 50/50 representation in parliament. She advises men not to be scared that women want to be in the highest decision making body in the country – politics.

"We encourage fathers (our husbands) to give us support we cannot be alone in this we need men to also support us. We have been advocating for women's representation in parliament as a lone voice. Isn't it nice to be called the husband of the President or Minister? My husband is happy to be the husband of a Councillor because he gets to know what is happening in our town/city. It is something to be proud about to know that your wife is one of the people bringing development to the city, which can only happen when a women is into active politics."

She is happy that her husband supports and encourages her, he even accompanies her to workshops and conferences to do with her work.

A veteran politicians **Emelda Maina Mandava** sums it all as she feels politics is also for women's self actualization.

"I encourage women to be involved in politics. It helps women in general and the woman politician herself. As a woman politician you become knowledgeable about a lot of things, your horizons broaden by being in politics. I would like to give as an example that it is because of being a politician that is why I am in COPAC, which will help me as a person and also to help others. It helps me with my confidence, dignity and when you see me, *"Handiti munoti Senator vasvika, ehe zvinondipawo self actualization"* (When you see me you say the Senetor is here, it gives me self actualization).

Now that women know better, we hope they will vote other women into parliament and support each other.

It is important to have women in key positions, in the forefront in the running of the country, the fact that they are women in decision making benefits other women, as they have the opportunity to actually shape and influence decisions on how the country is run.

GENDER DESEGREGATED DATA FOR THE PARLIAMENTOF ZIMBABWE SINCE 1980 - 2013

Elections and Appointments	Seats	Men	Women	% Of Women
1980	40	37	3	7.5
1990	150	133	17	11.3
1995	150	136	21	14
2000	150	136	14	9.3
2005	216	168	48	22.22
2009	210	178	32	16.1

The feature is an extract from the book –*History of Women Politicians in Zimbabwe* and *Women's Histories in Zimbabwe Book* by Joyce Jenje Makwenda

JULY

SUN	MON	TUES	WED	THUR	FRI	SAT

Maposhere Darcus (ZANU PF - MP Gokwe)

DARCUS Maposhere was born in 1960 in Chiredzi but her family moved to Gokwe. She was a collaborator during the war (chimbwido). She was chosen by 5 wards to represent them as MP.

As a female parliamentarian, she feels women at grassroots level feel free to talk to her about any issues affecting them, rather than talking to men. The challenge facing many women in parliament is confidence, but with regular workshops, Darcus feels that her confidence is improving. She also feels that many women do not want to get involved in politics because of fear of being labeled; but that does not deter her, and she wants more women to get involved and promote each other.

She started youth tournaments and competition and winners get T-shirts. She is also working with women at ward level.

NOTES

NOTES

NOTES

128

NOTES

130

Masaiti Evelyn (MDC-T - MP for Dzivarasekwa; MDC National Executive)

EVELYN Masaiti, nee Muzungu, was born in Bikita in 1965, and was an active ZANU PF supporter till 1999 when she joined the MDC and became MP for Mutasa constituency after a campaign marred by political violence in which her village and property were burnt to ashes. She also faced challenges at primary elections because of her tribe (Karanga) campaigning in Mutasa (Manyika). In 2008 she was elected MP for Dzivarasekwa and Deputy Minister of Women Affairs, Gender and Community Development from 2009 till June 2010. She is in the MDC National Executive.

Evelyn urges all women to rise above party politics and work together, and feels that organizations like WIPSU and Women's Trust are making major contributions to help women become confident.

She believes that educating women is educating the nation while educating a man is educating an individual. She wants Zimbabwe to fulfill the Gender protocol of 50/50 representation by 2015. She feels that without proper implementation programme the new Gender and Domestic Violence Act is ineffective, and she wants women to be uplifted socially, politically and economically.

Masuku Angeline: Matebeleland South Provincial Governor & Politburo Secretary for Gender and Culture

ANGELINE Masuku was born in 1936, and was appointed Governor and Resident Minister for Matabeleland South in November 2003. She served as MP for Luveve constituency from 1990 to 1995, and is also the Secretary for the disabled in the ZANU (PF) Politburo. She vows to work with the people in her Province to ensure that her term as Governor is successful. She believes in youths' empowerment since they are the fore bearers of the country's heritage and resources. She discourages parents and politicians from using the youth during campaigns and turning them into hooligans. She educates people in her area on political education, "I tell that we can differ politically but let us bring up our children in a manner that will shape them into good leaders of tomorrow."

She supports animal husbandry projects in Matabeleland to boost cattle population, and irrigation since the food security of the people of Matabeleland depends on irrigation projects. Matabeleland is generally a dry area with low rainfall pattern.

Masuku believes that as a female Governor she has to work a lot harder than her male colleagues to be recognized, a challenge that she is taking by the horns.

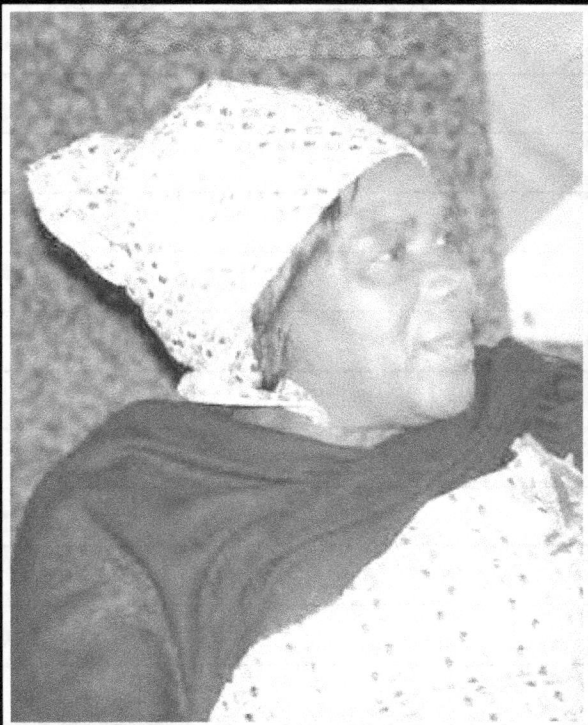

Matamisa Editor (MDC – T- Kadoma Central)

EDITOR Matamisa, nee Tsomondo, who is the MDC MP for Kadoma, was born in Hwedza. She went to St Anne's Mission where the late Minister Mahachi was the school head-boy at the time. She was married in 1971, took care of her siblings after her father died, and trained as a teacher at Mkoba together with her husband, after she studied for O' and A' Levels through correspondence. She also studied for BA and Masters Degrees with Zimbabwe Open University. Because of her ability to challenge oppression, she was encouraged by her younger son to join politics, and represented the MDC in the 2000 mayoral elections.

She was elected the MDC Women's Coordinator in 2005 and MP in 2008.

Notes

AUGUST

SUN	MON	TUES	WED	THUR	FRI	SAT

Matibenga Lucia (MDC-T
MP for Kuwadzana,
Governing Member of
the International Labour
Organisation)

LUCIA Gladys Matibenga, Minister of Public Service was born in Bulawayo and went to school at St Francis of Assisi in Chivhu. The late Josiah Tongogara was her husband's first cousin (not brother as some people believe). During the war she mobilized resources for freedom-fighters operating in Chirumanzu, Shurugwi, and Chivi. She married one of the freedom-fighters who became one of the 12   MPs representing Zanu Pf in Midlands Province from 1980-1985. He died in 1990 and was buried at Gweru Provincial Heroes Acre. She ceased to support Zanu Pf in 1986 after her husband was dropped from leadership position due to inter-party fighting.

Matibenga's activism continued in 1981 when she joined a trade union and represented workers working in shops, and challenged the oppression of African workers. She later joined the ZCTU, becoming its Vice President in 2003. Recently she was elected in absentee in Geneva to be a governing member of the International Labour Organisation. Lucia challenges the exclusion of women in central governing bodies, and believes that Women's Leagues, which perform as auxiliary bodies, oppress women because most of their members have been in the League since they were formed. She wants the women's organizations to become factories of leadership for women to be incorporated into main stream organizations. In MDC mainstream body there are only two women. Women in leadership should also serve as role models to encourage other women to join. She was impressed by women in Sudan Parliament who discuss real issues such as managing diversity in Africa.

Matienga Margaret
(MDC- MP for Sunningdale)

MARGARET Matienga was born in Harare in 1956 and grew up in Mbare. In 1974 she tried to cross into Mozambique to join the liberation struggle but was captured at the border and served three months in Chikurubhi Prison. She operated in Musana as a collaborator, travelling with freedom fighters carrying their weapons and cooking food until independence when she went into Assembly Points. She later joined the National Union of Clothing Industries Trade Union. She was instrumental in the formation of MDC. She became a ward councilor for Mbare but later resigned in solidarity with the suspension of Mayor Mudzuri.

Margaret experienced in-fighting within the party, especially from women. She also felt let down by WIPSU when she requested money for fuel during her campaign, but got help from Women's Trust and other well-wishers. As an MP she feels that female MPs from both parties are united, but it is difficult to make individual decisions because of party whipping system. Margaret wants more women into politics because they are focused and less corrupt than men. "If a man wants to fight a woman he uses another woman and it's very strong because if a woman fights you, she fights you..."she says, and encourages women to be strong, work together and support each other.

Mathuthu Thokozile (Governor Matabeleland North)

The late THOKOZILE MATHUTHU was born on 26 March, 1957 in Bulawayo. She worked as a temporary teacher, wages clerk, manager designate, district co-ordinator and administration manager for different companies since 1973. In 2001, she became the ZANU PF Politburo Secretary for Transport and Social Welfare. She was appointed Matabeleland North Province Governor and Resident Minister in 2005. She was also the Secretary for Transport and Social Welfare in the ZANU PF Women's League.

Mathuthu was a committee member in the ZANU PF Politburo. In her political career, she actively participated during the Liberation War as a member of the Unarmed Resistance Force. She rose from housing ZIPRA forces during the Liberation War to holding several positions in the PF ZAPU Women's Wing and Governor for Matabeleland North Province.

She was a well – organized and reliable person, possessing a good sense of humour and the ability to communicate comfortably with people at all levels. She worked well as a team member.

NOTES

NOTES

NOTES

NOTES

NOTES

147

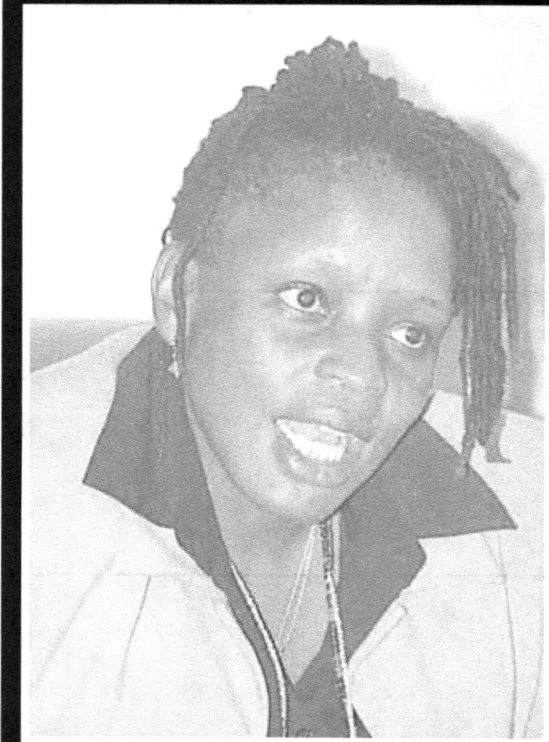

Misihairabwi-Mushonga Priscilla (MDC - Minister of Regional Integration and International Cooperation).

PRISCILLA Misihairabwi-Mushonga is a champion for women's rights, and is the only female negotiator in the GPA. She was elected MP for Glen Norah in 2000, after an election marred by political violence, and she believes that women should never have to be exposed to any violence of some sort.

"unfortunately the people that bore the brunt of that violence were women... either in actually being physically beaten but because women have problem reporting even to the status quo, or being able to expose themselves to the media their stories went unreported, the same thing with cases of rape we know that a lot of sexual abuse reigning and we know how it is with sexual abuse and women coming out and saying you know I've been sexually abused not many women can actually do that"

Priscilla was appointed Minister of Regional Integration and International Cooperation, in the government of national unity, in the 2009. She is the MDC party Secretary General and MDC chief representative at JOMIC (Joint Monitoring and Implementation Committee) and COPAC the Constitutional Parliamentary Committee a committee in charge of writing the Zimbabwean constitution.

Mlothswa Sthembile
(MDC - T — Senator for Matobo).

SITHEMBILE Mlothswa (nee Sibanda) started politics when she was very young in Matopos. She joined the MDC and rose through the ranks, to the National Executive. The party asked her to become an MP for Matobo in 2008, and she won because she connected well with people from all wards.

"I don't regret to be a woman, I don't like to compete like a man, no, I want to be myself and yes, my contribution should be taken as a contribution from a person and not as a woman," she says.

She believes that the benefits of being a female in Parliament are the same as those of a man; because to be a leader of people one has to understand them.

There are more women than men in the country, and men do not understand what women want, and only guess what women need because they are not women.

"When women complain of something like maternity leave you feel it as a woman because you are part of it. As a woman you want to make policies which will help alleviate the problems faced by women and yourself because you know how it feels."

Notes

SEPTEMBER

SUN	MON	TUES	WED	THUR	FRI	SAT

Mohadi Tambudzani (ZANU PF - Senator for Beitbridge)

TAMBUDZANI Mohadi was born to a family of politics. Her father, Mleya, was arrested and imprisoned for life at Chikurubi as a D class prisoner. Her husband also went to war in 1972 and came back in 1980. Tambudzani became a Senator 2005, although she says she did not want to be a Senator because her husband was already an MP in the area, and did not want it to look like a family thing.

Mohadi practices what she preaches, and has groomed a number of women into politics in her area. She believes that most women fail to understand politics because they do not have idols to look up to. Women in Beitbridge, the border town of Zimbabwe and South Africa, are grateful to have Mama Mohadi as she is affectionately known in her area. Her political career is deeply rooted in her community. At community level she has been involved in a number of projects while she was working for Agritex and then Lutheran. It is through this community work that her constituency asked her to stand and represent them.

She encourages women to engage in self-help projects, more so if they are in politics, and believes that women are still oppressed by society; and that it will be very difficult to achieve 50/50 representation since at the moment they do not even have 30% representation.

Mpariwa Paurina (MDC-T – Minister of Labour and Social Welfare, MP for Mufakose)

A FORMER OK Bazaars employee, Paurina Mpariwa's political activism started through trade unions, first representing OK workers in the Commercial workers Union until she joined the ZCTU. She became the first woman to be elected Chairperson of the Women's Council (ZCTU) in 1999.

She was one of the founding members of the MDC. Paurina is the party's secretary for Labour, and she has the women, most who are involved in the vibrant informal sector, and youths, at her heart. She is concerned about the high levels of unemployment.

Mpariwa is constantly liaising with the ZCTU on the welfare of these women and youth. Mpariwa looks to a future where the economic stability and integrity of Zimbabwe is restored and there is a more equitable distribution of resources. In October 2003, Pauline was elected to the Pan African Parliament, and is still is a member.

NOTES

154

NOTES

NOTES

NOTES

NOTES

Mtingwende Tariro (ZANU PF – Senator for Gokwe North)

TARIRO Mtingwende was born in Nembudziya, Gokwe North, in 1959. She joined politics after 1980, and became the District Chair Person for Gokwe North (ZANU PF). She had a passion for women issues, and wanted to make changes to their lives. She believes that it is important for women to join politics and participate in decision making because they are familiar with issues affecting them; including political violence and rape, while men can easily sneak away when things get tough.

Campaigning in the primaries was not easy for her. She lost to a man because she did not have enough resources. However, with the support of her District, she later campaigned to be a Senator and won. She believes that she was successful in her election because she worked well with people, especially women, because she had initiated many projects for women and youths.

Mtingwende believes that it is important for women to be in Parliament because most constituencies represented by women tend to do better than those represented by men. Tariro is happy that her husband supports her, unlike most women who may want to advance in politics but their husbands hold them back especially when they feel threatened.

Muchena Olivia (ZANU PF – Minster of Women's Affairs)

OLIVIA Muchena was born in Mtoko in 1946 to politically conscious parents. She is a cabinet member, and Minister of Women's Affairs. Her father would sacrifice buying his children a loaf of bread to buy a newspaper so as to keep track of political issues and current affairs.

To her, politics is not only interesting and challenging, but keeps her mind, body and soul busy. She believes that having more women in parliament will help to address gender imbalances. Although women maybe interested in politics, their participation is limited by   social, cultural and economic factors. She believes 50/50 representation will be achieved through constitutional, legislative and educational measures.

Olivia has a PhD in Agriculture Extension Education from Iowa State University

Muchenje Virginia (ZANU PF - Senator for Zvimba)

VIRGINIA Muchenje started participating in politics in the mid 70s. She became awakened to gender activism since many parents during that time preferred to send the male-child to school, and the government had laws that oppressed women. Women were not allowed to apply for ID cards, or to vote. When she opened a Bank Account she had to ask her brother who was four years younger than her, to open the account. Women were also not allowed to apply for maternity leave. Women were also getting half salaries. As a temporary teacher she was getting paid £3.10 while a fellow male teacher was paid £7. During the war she supported the freedom fighters by giving them food, shelter and medicines.

After independence she became an active member of Zanu, working at grassroots level. She trained at Silveira House and Domboshava Training in Home Economics and Community Development in Rural Areas. She used the knowledge to work with women's projects to upgrade their lives. She wants maternity leave to increase to between 4 and 6 months with full pay because child bearing is a national duty. Virginia encourages women to pursue education because it creates opportunities to challenge oppression.

The number of female Councilors and Ministers will subsequently increase. Female councilors are more likely to focus on boreholes, clean water, clinics (welfare issues). In terms of campaigning, men tend to out-compete women because they have resources. They can also travel far and wide while the women are constrained by household commitments. These obstacles can be overcome if women are empowered financially through projects, and also through training in leadership skills. Women should also have access to loan.

Notes

OCTOBER

SUN	MON	TUES	WED	THUR	FRI	SAT

Muchihwa – Dandajena Rorana (MDC – T - Senator with 11 constituencies and 26 wards)

RORANA Dandajena's political activism dates back to 1966, and during the liberation war she worked with the freedom fighters as a collaborator, carrying their weapons and goods when they moved about in the country. However, she decided to join the MDC after the launch because of dissatisfaction with the government.

She was the Chairperson for Resident Association (CRA). She faced political violence and was attacked and humiliated by female opponents. Rorana believes women can be each other's enemy, and pull each other down a lot. In her political struggle she experienced more violence from women than men; although she also admits that she gained support from women's organizations like Wipsu.

She believes that women need to be educated to respect and love themselves. "50/50 cannot be achieved if women don't respect and love each other".

NOTES

NOTES

172

NOTES

NOTES

Muchinguri Oppah (Secretary of the Women's League in Zanu PF; Politburo member, and war veteran).

OPPAH Muchinguri was born in 1958, and joined the liberation war and received military training in guerilla warfare in Mozambique. She prides in the role played by women during the liberation war "I am a politburo member, but I'm also a war veteran who fought side by side with men...Women's emancipation did not just come without a price. We went through the war of liberation where we lost sons and daughters of Zimbabwe...It was not the easiest thing for us women in Zimbabwe..." she said, at a 50/50 representation workshop held in Harare on 3 August 2011.

She believes that women participation in decision making is the key to women's development. "We have witnessed countries like South Africa performing so well to ensure that there are more women in decision-making. Same for Mozambique, and other countries...we have now decided as women of Zimbabwe that we need to speak with one voice," She continued.

Oppah feels that although Zimbabwe has almost 19 pieces of legislation in favour of women, more needs to be done in terms of implementation, including allocation of land to women, where 16% only of the land has been distributed to women. Muchinguri believes that economic empowerment for women will only be achieved if women stand up and fight for a gender balance; including "increased participation in the educational system, political decision making workforce, and the more women become economically independent the less they are likely to remain living in difficult situations in their families, discriminatory workplaces and in unhappy marriages." Oppah held many portfolios after independence. She was the Deputy Minister of State for External Affairs from 1989-93; and Minister of Women's Affairs, Gender and Community Development from 2005 to 2009 among other portfolios.

MUDAU Metrine
(MDC-T - MP Beitbridge West)

METRINE Mudau was the first female Councilor in Beitbridge, and acknowledges that she joined politics after Mama Mohadi, who was the first female Senator, encouraged women to be in politics. She chaired the Beitbridge Council before becoming an MP. Her place (as a councilor) was filled by another woman. Beitbridge has six female Councilors. "To be a good politician one has to go and meet others and learn what they do...the workshops by WIPSU have helped us that politics is not for men only," she says.

Metrine believes that she won both the primaries (against two women and the men) and against the MDC candidate because she had the support of women, who are no longer afraid of voting another woman. With the CDF money, she extended the clinic and built a house for nurses, although she would have wanted to build a school so that children would not have to walk long distances to get to school. She gets support from her husband Major Madau, and does not feel intimidated to talk in parliament. "You don't go into politics because you have a degree, but because of the work that one does with the community, so there are certain things that I do not understand and he [husband] helps me."

Metrine married her husband in 1975, before he left to join the war but she waited for him. She wants Parliament to enact laws that punish rapists severely, including life behind bars. When a woman gets into parliament, it helps other women to get access to information, because women like to share [information].

179

Mujuru Joice (ZANU – PF - Incumbent Vice President of Zimbabwe, MP Mount Darwin West)

JOICE Mujuru was born Runaida Mugari in 1955 in Mt Darwin, and left Zimbabwe (then Rhodesia) for military training in 1973. She returned to Zimbabwe briefly in 1974 (battlefront). Joice assumed the name Teurai Ropa during the war, which became Teurai Ropa Nhongo after she married the late Solomon Mujuru (Rex Nhongo). In Mozambique she became a military trainer, and was the only female combatant to be an army commander. She was Zimbabwe's first and youngest woman to have served as a Cabinet Minister in 1980 when she was appointed Minister of Youth, Education and Culture. She has since then held several ministerial posts. VP Mujuru believes all women should work for leadership roles and be accepted by men as leaders.

As a young woman Joice did not believe that boys were stronger than girls. "She did not believe in the boy child being stronger or better than the girl child. Her belief was that we are all the same in the eyes of God. She is a real leader that one," said Shepherd, VP Mujuru's brother. Her mother Ambuya Mugari also said that although Joice was assertive as a young child, "Obedience was her trademark and remains so to this day."

VP Mujuru commands respect from people around her. She is humble, and a torch-bearer not only for Zimbabwean people, but for women especially and the Korekore people. "I saw Teurai grow into the woman she is. Ndakaona humhandara hwake. Nhasi ndinefara kuti ndezveduwo kumaKorekore tava naVP," said Chief Kandeya. "She is like a queen to us. We consider her to be just like a queen."

Zanu PF Provincial Chairman (Mashonaland West) Mr Edion Chiripanyanga said of VP Mujuru, "I worked with her soon after independence and I must say I do not want to hear the gender balance argument. We do not approve of her nomination as a woman but because she is an able and deserving leader. She is a friendly yet stern woman and in her we have chosen as able a leader as President Mugabe himself."

('Quote from -**The Sunday Mail** 24 November 2004 by Robert Mukondiwa - *The rise of Joyce Mujuru*).

NOVEMBER

SUN	MON	TUES	WED	THUR	FRI	SAT

Mutsvangwa Monica (ZANU – PF – MP Chimanimani)

MONICA Mutsvangwa has been in politics since the age of 15 when she left the country to join the liberation struggle. Mutsvangwa would like to take a rather different approach to the usual and would like women to also involve men by educating them as they need to be enlightened. "But it's all about educating men, if you leave them out thinking that they know, how do they know? They have been brought up by us and we also, because of the cultural society that says this is for men and this for women, we just have to educate them."

Some of her responsibilities in parliament are as follows; she is part of the 25 select Committee Members who are spearheading COPAC, and she is the co-Vice Chair. She is the Chairperson of the portfolio committee on indigenization and empowerment which entails a lot of work. A delegate of the SADC Parliamentary forum and there she was Treasurer for the Executive for 2 years. She is also a technical advisor when it comes to reading bills to members of her party ZANU PF.

Mutsvangwa encourages women to be active in politics than to criticize from an aloof position. "I feel we need to really get away from the idea of sitting back and reading and watching news and going on internet and then critisice. We need to do something as Zimbabweans and especially when we talk of women, we can never attain the 50/50 if women do not get out of that home and say look I need to participate in politics, we need women to get out there, it is so sad for a country which has had so many good policies about education to install few highly educated women in Parliament.

NOTES

NOTES

NOTES

NOTES

Ncube Spiwe (MDC-T Senator for Emganwini).

SPIWE Ncube started political activism through trade unionism, and was one of the founding members of the MDC. She was elected as the Vice Organizing Secretary at the launch of MDC, and is in the MDC National Executive Committee. Spiwe acknowledges that being in politics has helped her to rise as a woman.

"Working as a politician is not easy but one has to be brave, one has to be sure of themselves, believing in yourself is very important if one has to be in politics and you should know what you want. You should not worry about what other people say about you ..." she says.

Spiwe says her husband is very supportive.

She feels that women are now fighting each other, instead of supporting each other. She would like to be given another term in Parliament to see her current projects reap fruits.

"We have done (projects) that we still want to see to the end if we could get the chance to go on we could achieve our goals. If we can have two terms but what is important is that as women we should support each other," Spiwe says.

She acknowledges that some of the challenges that she faces comes from her own party. "...fighting each other is very retrogressive in a Party...if we don't achieve 50/50 across the board then it will not be achieved in politics. We might end up fighting for political positions as women and yet there is so much to do and there other areas where we can go and be leaders, these areas can be feeders for politics."

Anastancia Ndhlovu
(ZANU PF - MP for
Shurugwi)

ANASTANCIA Ndhlovu is the youngest MP for Zanu PF. She was born on 6 October, 1980 in Shurugwi, and attended Charles Wraith Primary School in Shurugwi and Thornhill High School. She has a BSc Honours in Human Resources Management from the Midlands State University, and currently studying for an MSc in Human Resources Management. Anastancia is the National Deputy Secretary for Administration in the ZANU PF Youth League. She is the First Vice President – World Federation of Democratic Youth (WFDY). She is also a Human Resources Specialist – ZIMRA. She was elected Member of Parliament during the 2008 elections.

Anastancia hailed the Constituency Development Fund, but believes that rural areas should be awarded more money because they are large and have diverse needs different from urban areas. She used hers on a number of projects, including community empowerment projects targeting women.

"The projects have changed many people's livelihoods especially in the area of education and health care," she says.

Ndlovhu Patricia (ZANU PF - Councilor for Beitbridge)

"EVERYTHING that we do is politics, even if we may choose not to believe it. Wherever you walk its politics! The water that you drink is politics!" said Patricia Ndlovu, the only woman councillor in Beitbridge, who feels why it is important for women to be in politics as councillors and parliamentarians. She would like to encourage men to support their wives to be in politics, as women politicians are working towards 50/50 representation in parliament. She advises men not to be scared that women want to be in the highest decision making body in the country – politics. Councillor Ndlovu is part of the team that has brought development to Beitbridge, a border post town which borders Zimbabwe and South Africa.

"We encourage fathers (our husbands) to give us support we cannot be alone in this we need men to also support us. We have been advocating for women's representation in parliament as a lone voice. Isn't it nice to be called the husband of the President or Minister? My husband is happy to be the husband of a Councillor because he gets to know what is happening in our town/city. It is something to be proud about to know that your wife is one of the people bringing development to the city, which can only happen when a women is into active politics."

She is happy that her husband supports and encourages her, he even accompanies her to workshops and conferences to do with her work.

The councillor feels that at ward level there should be more women councillors and this will open the room for more female mayors; because mayors are voted by councillors and male councillors are likely to vote for male mayors.

DECEMBER

SUN	MON	TUES	WED	THUR	FRI	SAT

Nyamupinga Biata Beatrice
(ZANU PF - Chairwoman
Women's Parliamentarian Caucus
– Goromonzi MP)

BIATA Nyamupinga feels that through Wipsu workshops many women are becoming more confident even to speak in front of intellectuals. She wants 50/50 representation to be achieved by 2015, and to start in Parliament because "that's where policies are made, and that's where favourable policies for women can be enacted".

Currently there are only 33 women out of 210 in the House of Assembly (representing on 1% out of 52% of the population into leadership).

"We remain poor and when we are poor, elections have been commercialized, we will lose them but if we are economically empowered we will achieve because it is easy when you have resources", she says.

Biata believes that because women are marginalized and outnumbered in Parliament, it is easy for male MPs to reject any constitutional proposal which favour women, hence 105 seats should be reserved for women.

NOTES

NOTES

NOTES

NOTES

Nyoni Stembiso (ZANU PF – Minister of Medium and Small Scale Enterprises, MP Nkayi North)

"Politics is a game that our mothers never taught us, our mothers taught us to care, to share and to serve. In fact my own mother, what I really got from her are those 3 values, so when you get into politics you find that there is so much that is strange to you, where positions sometimes matter more than loving, caring and serving each other. So as a woman you have to adjust, you have to create your space and say within this space I will use these values that my mother taught me to get into power, if you don't do that you lose your womanhood, you lose your values and then you don't make the impact into politics and therefore I would have missed something in leadership if I hadn't come into politics. Politics has taught me to be my own woman regardless of what and I have gone through, I have lost elections, I have won elections but all I have done is I have been myself in whatever I have done," said Sithembiso Nyoni, a woman who has been in politics for almost 20 years and is interested in development, her slogan is 'Zenzele', a Ndebele word for do it for yourself, as development can never be given and cannot be imposed on the people, it has to be a force from inside that is watered and guided and assisted to grow.

Her speeches are about issues, about development and this has become her brand. Hon Nyoni believes that you can be a politician and still maintain your integrity.

Sthembiso Nyoni believes that through unity, women can achieve 50/50 representation in parliament.

"Rwanda has done it, Rwanda has surpassed this so yes it is possible", she says.

Sandi-Ndlovu Eunice (ZANU PF - Politburo Member)

"IT'S good for women to venture into politics because politics decides the way a country should go, so women must be a part of that decision-making process but unfortunately sometimes personal egos hamper this set-up. We sometimes become too greedy, sometimes we want to challenge each other over nothing. I believe we should focus with the agenda of promoting women in the manner that it should be, the manner is don't challenge a woman who is already in a position, get the positions that the men are holding so that you become more in the set-up. What is the point of having 10 women out of 160 men, it does not work, then you go there and you fight for those 10 posts." Words of advice come from a veteran politician Eunice Sandi whose political career spans 5 decades.

While the women's wing is good for development, she encourages women that it should not keep them away from the male domain especially during elections." You are there, you are fixed up, at a corner somewhere doing your own thing as women, that's why we are still challenging each other so much and because of that we are not getting there."

Sandi was born in Zimbabwe in 1946 but grew up in South Africa, where she trained as a teacher. She returned to teach in Zimbabwe in 1960, and joined ZAPU. She was also involved in the Trade Union movement. She went to Zambia in 1975 where she trained as a soldier, and was sent to Germany to train in reconnaissance. She was a broadcaster for ZAPU.

She is the founder of an NGO Women In Business in the 1980'. She worked in Nkomo's (Father Zimbabwe) office after independence, and is a politburo member for Zanu PF, and the Deputy Secretary for Women's League. She became Senator for Plumtree from 2006-2008.

Shirichena Elina (ZANU PF - MP for Mberengwa South)

ELINA Shirichena started politics around 1975. She worked for 10 years under the Ministry of Women's Affairs in Community development, before she became a provincial chairwoman, councilor and now MP. Women chose her to represent them because she used to work with them doing some empowering projects.

Her husband did not want her to join politics because he thought it was good for single women, but the community leaders convinced him and he now supports her. Shirichena was groomed by Wipsu to become confident and develop leadership skills.

She works with 65 young women that she groomed who help her to run the constituency even in her absence. She empowered the young women financially through self-help projects so that they become confident. She believes that to achieve 50/50 women should join political parties of their choice and rise through the structures, and those women need to be united to implement projects and laws which benefit them.

Notes

JANUARY

SUN	MON	TUES	WED	THUR	FRI	SAT

Sibanda – Mloyi Agnes (MDC-T - Senator for Gwabalanda)

AGNES Mloyi (nee Sibanda) was born in Godlwayo, but grew up in Kezi (same place with Joshua Nkomo) at a place called Dombodombo. She was a Zapu activist and rose through the structures of the party till she became District Chairperson for ZAPU. However, she later joined the MDC at its inception, becoming the first Interim District Chair for Women (Luveve), and later the   Provincial Chairwoman (Women's Assembly).

"When there was a split in the MDC in 2005, it was us the women who made sure that the party did not die. When we had a congress I was elevated to the Main, so I was the one leading the Main Province in Bulawayo."

She became a Senator in 2008. She believes that in politics one has to be brave, and that men don't think a woman can lead. She was the only woman who was leading a Province. She also believes that women can pull each other down, and that if there are more women in parliament they can pass bills that are favourable to women, and deny those that oppress women. However, she thinks the main problem with women is that most of them are not educated, while the educated ones do not want to be involved in politics.

"We have been asking educated women to join us than to criticize us by saying uneducated people don't know anything and yet the educated don't want to join politics; the bottom line is that we do not support each other," she says.

Sibanda Dorcas (MDC T - MP for Bulawayo Central and Parliament's Deputy Chief Whip)

FORTY-five-year-old Dorcas Sibanda was born in Tshabalala, Bulawayo. She joined ZAPU during the colonial era, and the MDC in 1999 through a Trade Union, Zimbabwe Association of Railway Union (ZARU). She rose through the ranks, and was elected MP for Bulawayo Central in 2008, and also a Deputy Chief Whip in Parliament. Confident to move motions and participate in debates, Dorcas acknowledges that at times resentment comes from fellow women parliamentarians.

She is a single mother to four daughters aged between nine and twenty-eight. Politics runs in her family. Her father, Gowe Sibanda, was an active ZAPU member, while her three brothers were ZIPRA fighters.

She believes empowering a woman is empowering a whole nation.

Stevenson Trudy (former MDC MP for Harare North)

GERTRUDE Stevenson was born in the USA in 1944, and describes herself as a war-baby. Her father was a northerner while her mother was a southerner, and there was antagonism between people of the north with people of the south then. She was therefore enlightened to political consciousness and human rights at an early age. Her mother was not fully accepted by her father's family.

She was the MDC MP for Harare North Constituency from 2000 to 2008, and is currently a member of the National Education Advisory Board. A human and women's rights activist, she has founded a number of organizations.

Gertrude moved to England with her mother where she later graduated with a degree at the University of Reading. With her husband Stewart Stevenson, the couple travelled to Uganda in 1969 and left in 1972, and went to settle in Swaziland where Stevenson taught at a primary school. From 1976-78 they were in Zambia, and after a short period living in Rome, they came to Zimbabwe in 1980 shortly after the nation celebrated its independence. Stevenson taught French and Italian at an elite private girl's school, Arundel Secondary School. Her life changed dramatically in 1988 when her husband left her.

"This is when I understood women's problems, as my husband left me poor and I had to look after three children," she said. "It was difficult to serve him with divorce notices as we did not know where he was until we found him in 1992, and the divorce went through."

Stevenson loved her adopted nation and acquired Zimbabwean citizenship in 1989, and plunged into women's and civic politics issues.

Zinyemba Margaret (ZANU PF - MP for Chiweshe)

MARGARET Zinyemba was born February 1939, and as a girl child her parents sent her younger brother to school (patriarchy) before her, and this helped to shape her activism as she sought to challenge gender imbalances and racism. She served Mazowe Rural District Council for 16 years as a Councilor. She was chosen by a delegation of men in her area to become an MP. Her constituency was reserved for women, so she stood against three women at primaries. Margaret acknowledges that the current political field poses challenges to women who want to engage in politics, because people nominate themselves, and there is also bribery and corruption (vote buying). There is now too much competition, which threatens women's unity. Women also lack resources (financial) to launch successful campaigns against men. However, she believes that it is important to have more women MPs because women are naturally nation builders, and in transparency and honest. She tells people in her constituency the truth about what she can achieve and what she cannot.

Through the Constituency Development Fund Margaret assisted schools and clinics in her constituency with resources. She also bought sports kits for children in schools to encourage physical fitness through sport, and helped some people to access loans for agriculture. She wants to develop roads (infrastructure) in her area to make some places accessible. She is also helping women to form clubs, as well as to help people in her constituency to apply for prospecting mining licenses. She wants more women to engage in politics and wants more female parliamentarians as this is the only way that women can challenge oppression and improve their welfare.

A message for women is that they should not let poverty decided their fate, because men can exploit that to their advantage.

213

Name..

Address...

....

Phone... Fax ....

Name..

Address...

....

Phone... Fax ....

Name..

Address...

....

Phone... Fax ....

Name..

Address...

....

Phone... Fax ....

Name...

Address...

....

Phone.. Fax ....

Name...

Address...

....

Phone.. Fax ....

Name...

Address...

....

Phone.. Fax ....

Name...

Address...

....

Phone.. Fax ....

Name..

Address..

....

Phone... Fax ....

Name..

Address..

Phone... Fax ....

Name..

Address..

....

Phone... Fax ....

Name..

Address..

....

Phone... Fax ....

Name..

Address..

....

Phone... Fax ....

Name..

Address..

Phone... Fax ....

Name..

Address..

....

Phone... Fax ....

Name..

Address..

....

Phone... Fax ....

Name...

Address..

....

Phone.. Fax ....

Name...

Address..

....

Phone.. Fax ....

Name...

Address..

....

Phone.. Fax ....

Name...

Address..

....

Phone.. Fax ....

Name..

Address...

....

Phone.. Fax ....

Name..

Address...

Phone.. Fax ....

Name..

Address...

....

Phone.. Fax ....

Name..

Address...

....

Phone.. Fax ....

Name..

Address...

....

Phone.. Fax ....

Name..

Address...

Phone.. Fax ....

Name..

Address...

....

Phone.. Fax ....

Name..

Address...

....

Phone.. Fax ....

Name...

Address..

....

Phone.. Fax ....

Name...

Address..

Phone.. Fax ....

Name...

Address..

....

Phone.. Fax ....

Name...

Address..

....

Phone.. Fax ....

QR

Name..

Address...

....

Phone... Fax ....

Name..

Address...

Phone... Fax ....

Name..

Address...

....

Phone... Fax ....

Name..

Address...

....

Phone... Fax ....

Name..

Address...

....

Phone... Fax ....

Name..

Address...

Phone... Fax ....

Name..

Address...

....

Phone... Fax ....

Name..

Address...

....

Phone... Fax ....

Name..

Address...

....

Phone... Fax ....

Name..

Address...

Phone... Fax ....

Name..

Address...

....

Phone... Fax ....

Name..

Address...

....

Phone... Fax ....

XYZ

Name...

Address..

....

Phone... Fax ....

Name...

Address..

Phone... Fax ....

Name...

Address..

....

Phone... Fax ....

Name...

Address..

....

Phone... Fax ....

Credits

JANUARY		COMMISSIONED	
NAME	RESEARCH/INTERVIEW	PHOTOGRAPHER	ADAPTATION/EDITING
Bhudha Masara	Joyce Jenje Makwenda	Fidelis Zvomuya	Sarudzayi Chifamba Barnes
Sibusisiwe Bhuka Flora	*Source:* Zimbawe Parliament Website		
	Dumisani Muleya	Fidelis Zvomuya	Sarudzayi Chifamba Barnes
	thezimbabweindepenedent.com, herald.com, afdevinfo.com		
Chabuka Keresenzia	Joyce Jenje Makwenda	Fidelis Zvomuya	Sarudzayi Chifamba Barnes
Chaderopa Fungai	Joyce Jenje Makwenda	Fidelis Zvomuya	Sarudzayi Chifamba Barnes
Chibhagu Gertrude	Joyce Jenje Makwenda	Fidelis Zvomuya	Sarudzayi Chifamba Barnes

FEBRUARY			
Chikava Betty	Joyce Jenje Makwenda	Fidelis Zvomuya	Sarudzayi Chifamba Barnes
Chimbudzi Alice	Joyce Jenje Makwenda	Fidelis Zvomuya	Sarudzayi Chifamba Barnes
Chinomona Mabel	Joyce Jenje Makwenda	Fidelis Zvomuya	Sarudzayi Chifamba Barnes
Chitsa Enna	Joyce Jenje Makwenda	Fidelis Zvomuya	Sarudzayi Chifamba Barnes
Chung Fay	*Source;* Weiss 1986,		
	Envisions Zimbabwe	Dr. Fay Chung	Sarudzayi Chifamba Barnes
	Margaret Dongo		

MARCH			
Dete Agnes	Joyce Jenje Makwenda	Fidelis Zvomuya	Sarudzayi Chifamba Barnes
Dongo Margaret	Joyce Jenje Makwenda	Margaret Dongo	Sarudzayi Chifamba Barnes
Dube-Gombami Gladys	Joyce Jenje Makwenda	Fidelis Zvomuya	Sarudzayi Chifamba Barnes
Prof Gaidzanwa Rudo	*Source:* kubatana.net-	Fidelis Zvomuya	Sarudzayi Chifamba Barnes
	Envison Zimbabwe Women's Trust		
Goto Rosemary	Joyce Jenje Makwenda	Fidelis Zvomuya	Sarudzayi Chifamba Barnes

APRIL			
Holland Sekai	*Source:* Wikipedia,	Jeff Milanzi	Sarudzayi Chifamba Barnes
	Lance Guma 9/092010		
Karenyi Lynette	Joyce Jenje Makwenda	Fidelis Zvomuya	Sarudzayi Chifamba Barnes
Katsande Aqilina	Joyce Jenje Makwenda	Fidelis Zvomuya	Sarudzayi Chifamba Barnes
Katyamaenza Viriginia	Joyce Jenje Makwenda	Fidelis Zvomuya	Sarudzayi Chifamba Baranes
Khumalo Tabitha	Joyce Jenje Makwenda	Fidelis Zvomuya	Joyce Jenje Makwenda

MAY			
Khupe Thokozane	Joyce Jenje Makwenda	Fidelis Zvomuya	Sarudzayi Chifamba Barnes
	Additional Information: Speech at 50/50 Policy Relaunch 4/08/2011 countryoffice.unfpa.org		
Mabhiza Gladys	Joyce Jenje Makwenda	Fidelis Zvomuya	Sarudzayi Chifamba Barnes
Madzongwe Edna	Source: Herald 2004 Wikipedia, newzimbabwe.co 26/08/2008	Jeff Milanzi	Sarudzayi Chifamba Barnes
Mahofa Shuvai	Source: Herald 2004, The Standard 17/06/2007 – Walter Marwizi	Fidelis Zvomuya	Sarudzayi Chifamba Barnes
Mahoka Sarah	Joyce Jenje Makwenda	Fidelis Zvomuya	Sarudzayi Chifamba Barnes

Credits

JUNE

NAME	RESEARCH/INTERVIEW	COMMISSIONED PHOTOGRAPHER	ADAPTATION/EDITING
Majome Fungai Jessie	Joyce Jenje Makwenda	Fidelis Zvomuya	Sarudzayi Chfamba Barnes
Makone Theresa	John Gambanga, *Daily News*	Fidelis Zvomuya	John Gambanga
Mandaba Maina Imelda	Joyce Jenje Makwenda	Fidelis Zvomuya	Joyce Jenje Makwenda
Mangami Dorothy	Joyce Jenje Makwenda	Fidelis Zvomuya	Sarudzayi Chifamba Barnes
Manyeruke Jenia	Joyce Jenje Makwenda	Fidelis Zvomuya	Sarudzayi Chifamba Barnes
Feature	Written by Joyce Jenje Makwenda		

JULY

NAME	RESEARCH/INTERVIEW	COMMISSIONED PHOTOGRAPHER	ADAPTATION/EDITING
Maposhere Darcus	Joyce Jenje Makwenda	Fidelis Zvomuya	Sarudzayi Chifamba Barnes
Masaiti Evelyn	Joyce Jenje Makwenda	Fidelis Zvomuya	Sarudzayi Chifamba Barnes
Masuku Angeline	*Herald* 2004, Chronicle 22/12/2011	Wikipedia	Sarudzayi Chifamba Barnes
Matamisa Editor	Joyce Jenje Makwenda	Fidelis Zvomuya	Sarudzayi Chifamba Barnes

AUGUST

NAME	RESEARCH/INTERVIEW	COMMISSIONED PHOTOGRAPHER	ADAPTATION/EDITING
Matibenga Lucia	Joyce Jenje Makwenda	Fidelis Zvomuya	Sarudzayi Chifamba Barnes
Matienga Margaret	Joyce Jenje Makwenda	Fidelis Zvomuya	Sarudzayi Chifamba Barnes
Mathuthu Thokozile	www.afdevinfo.com,	Jeff Milanzi	www.copac.org.zw
Misihairabwi-Mushonga P	Joyce Jenje Makwenda Additional Information: Wikipedia		Sarudzayi Chifamba Barnes
Mlothswa Sthembile	Joyce Jenje Makwenda	Fidelis Zvomuya	Sarudzayi Chifamba Barnes

SEPTEMBER

NAME	RESEARCH/INTERVIEW	COMMISSIONED PHOTOGRAPHER	ADAPTATION/EDITING
Mohadi Tambudzai	Joyce Jenje Makwenda	Fidelis Zvomuya	Sarudzayi Chifamba Barnes
Mpariwa Paurina	Herald 2004, Wikipedia Zimsentinel.blogspot	Fidelis Zvomuya	Sarudzayi Chifamba Barnes
Mtingwende Tariro	Joyce Jenje Makwenda	Jeff Milanzi	Sarudzayi Chifamba Barnes
Muchena Olivia	Joyce Jenje Makwenda	Fidelis Zvomuya	Sarudzayi Chifamba Barnes
Muchenje Virginia	Joyce Jenje Makwenda	Fidelis Zvomuya	Sarudzayi Chifamba Barnes

OCTOBER

NAME	RESEARCH/INTERVIEW	COMMISSIONED PHOTOGRAPHER	ADAPTATION/EDITING
Muchihwa-D Rorana	Joyce Jenje Makwenda	Rorana Muchihwa	Sarudzayi Chifamba Barnes
Muchinguri Oppah	Speech at 50/50 Cummunique 3/08/2011 Wikipedia, Herald 13/03/2008	Fidelis Zvomuya	Sarudzayi Chifamba Barnes
Mudau Metrine	Joyce Jenje Makwenda	Fidelis Zvomuya	Sarudzayi Chifamba Barnes
Mujuru Joice	Wikipedia, *Sunday Mail* 24/11/2004 by Robert Mukondiwa		Sarudzayi Chifamba Barnes

NOVEMBER

NAME	RESEARCH/INTERVIEW	COMMISSIONED PHOTOGRAPHER	ADAPTATION/EDITING
Mutsvangwa Monica	Joyce Jenje Makwenda	Fidelis Zvomuya	Joyce Jenje Makwenda
Ncube Spiwe	Joyce Jenje Makwenda	Fidelis Zvomuya	Sarudzayi Chifamba Barnes
Ndlovu Anastancia	Joyce Jenje Makwenda	Jeff Milanzi	Sarudzayi Chifamba Barnes
Ndlovu Patricia	Joyce Jenje Makwenda	Fidelis Zvomuya	Joyce Jenje Makwenda

DECEMBER

NAME	RESEARCH/INTERVIEW	COMMISSIONED PHOTOGRAPHER	ADAPTATION/EDITING
Nyamupinga B Beatrice	Speech at 50/50 Relaunch Women's Views On News.Org	Fidelis Zvomuya	Sarudzayi Chifamba Barnes

Credits

DECEMBER		COMMISSIONED	
NAME	RESEARCH/INTERVIEW	PHOTOGRAPGHER	ADAPTATION/EDITING
Nyoni Sthembiso	Joyce Jenje Makwenda	Fidelis Zvomuya	Joyce Jenje Makwenda
Sandi-Ndlovu Eunice	Joyce Jenje Makwenda	Fidelis Zvomuya	Joyce Jenje Makwenda
Shirichena Elina	Joyce Jenje Makwenda	Fidelis Zvomuya	Joyce Jenje Makwenda
JANUARY			
Sibanda-Mloyi Agnes	Joyce Jenje Makwenda	Fidelis Zvomuya	Sarudzayi Chifamba Barnes
Stevenson Trudy	Joyce Jenje Makwenda		Sarudzayi Chifamba Barnes
Zinyemba Margaret	Joyce Jenje Makwenda	Fidelis Zvomuya	Sarudzayi Chifamba Barnes

Acknowledgements

SPECIAL THANKS To:
Joyce Jenje Makwenda Collection Archive (JJMCA), WIPSU Women In Politics Support Unit and Women of Africa Diary – for partly funding and facilitating the project. I would also like to thank Sarudzayi Chifamba for adapting and editing some of the transcribed interviews when I was busy with other work. All those who contributed to the success of the diary, thank you.

Publication credits

Creator/Director of Project/Research/ Interviews:	Joyce Jenje Makwenda
Assistant Coordinator/Researcher:	Yolanda Birivadi
Feature Story Writer:	Joyce Jenje Makwenda
Short stories Edit or:	Sarudzayi Chifamba Barnes
Editing:	Joyce Jenje Makwenda
Cover Design:	Joshua Sithole/Jeffrey Milanzi
Cover Photo front:	*Herald* – Joyce Mujuru and Thokozani Khupe
Cover Photo Back (Source):	Margaret Dongo – Margaret Dongo
Most of the photos:	Fidelis Zvomuya
Design and Layout:	Yolanda Birivadi
Design and Layout:	Jeffrey Milanzi

YOUR MENSTRUAL CHART

	JAN	FEB	MAR	APR	MAY	JUN	JUL	AUG	SEPT	OCT	NOV	DEC
1												
2												
3												
4												
5												
6												
7												
8												
9												
10												
11												
12												
13												
14												
15												
16												
17												
18												
19												
20												
21												
22												
23												
24												
25												
26												
27												
28												
29												
30												
31												

Notes

www.ingramcontent.com/pod-product-compliance
Lightning Source LLC
Chambersburg PA
CBHW052003270326
41929CB00015B/2770